THE LOST YEARS

By the same author

BELL' ANTONIO

e same author

ANTONIO

By t

BE

VITALIANO BRANCATI

The Lost Years

TRANSLATED FROM THE ITALIAN BY
PATRICK CREAGH

HARVILL
An Imprint of HarperCollins*Publishers*

First published in Italy serially in 1938 and in book form by
Valentino Bompiani, Milan, 1943
under the title *Gli Anni Perduti*
First published in Great Britain in 1992
by Harvill
an imprint of HarperCollins Publishers,
77/85 Fulham Palace Road,
Hammersmith, London W6 8JB

9 8 7 6 5 4 3 2 1

© 1987 Gruppo Editoriale Fabbri, Bompiani, Sonzogno, Etas S.p.A.
English translation © HarperCollins Publishers 1992

BRITISH LIBRARY CATALOGUING IN PUBLICATION DATA

Brancati, Vitaliano
The lost years.
I. Title II. Anni perduti. *English*
353.912 [F]

ISBN 0-00-271158-3

Set in Linotron Bembo by
Rowland Phototypesetting Ltd, Bury St Edmunds, Suffolk
Printed and bound in Great Britain by
Hartnolls Limited, Bodmin, Cornwall

Translator's Note

The Fascist regime, in power in Italy since 1922, made a marked change of pace in the years 1934–36. With internal opposition rigorously suppressed, Mussolini decided on a policy of expansion. The result was the brutal invasion of Abyssinia (1935–36), in which Italian forces, vastly better armed and not sparing in the use of mustard-gas, eventually overran the country and annexed it. This filthy piece of work was condemned as naked aggression by the League of Nations and world opinion in general, but it did less than nothing to harm Mussolini's personal image – to him "naked aggression" had a nice manly ring to it. It also encouraged like-minded people such as Hitler by proving that the League of Nations was powerless and that crime really paid. The Rome-Berlin Axis was formed in October in 1936, and the table was laid for the Second World War.

Vitaliano Brancati had joined the Fascist Party in 1924, at the age of 17, and he became no mere fellow-traveller of its ideology. "At twenty," he wrote, "I was a Fascist to the marrow of my bones. I seek for no extenuating circumstances for this. What attracted me in Fascism was all that was worst in it . . . and around my twentieth year I was frankly ashamed of all lofty and noble qualities and sought to debase and degrade myself with all the ingenuousness, eagerness and vehemence with which one may yearn for the contrary.".

These years in which Mussolini's regime was scaling new heights of militaristic fervour were the very ones in which Brancati turned from contributions to party-line publications (*"Lavoro fascista"*, *"Critica fascista"*, etc.), or works extolling the *Duce*, which were, so to speak, humourless by law, and put his hand to the composition of *The Lost Years*. Its publication began (1938) in the magazine *Omnibus*, which was suppressed the following year. The date of the copyright, 1943, the year of the Italian surrender to the Allies and the fall of Mussolini, is therefore misleading. *The Lost Years* was actually composed in the full flush of Fascist power and truculence, and during what, for Brancati, was a long period of painful soul-searching.

The purpose of this rather stodgy note is to convey something of why the book is the way it is. There is no open criticism of the regime, and no mention is made of any authority whatever with the exception of one obscure municipal clerk, but the apathy of almost all the characters is such as is induced by living under a despotism, and it takes an outsider, an "American", to galvanize them into an enterprise as lengthy and torpid as it is improbable and pointless. The book is a grotesque parable of futility, but I would not like to overstress the emblematic features of the story; merely to add that Brancati claimed this to be his first book, repudiating all previous work, and that in later life, when speaking of his Fascist period, he often called it his "lost years".

That Brancati is a *Sicilian* writer will be obvious to any reader of this fable. However, in his introduction to Brancati's collected works, the late Leonardo Sciascia points out that this Sicilian-ness will appear less evident, less "foreign", to real foreigners than to Italians. He writes: "The difficulty is not merely one of means – dialect, dialectal construction of sentences, references to traditions and customs, to historical pecularities; it is above all a difficulty of "sentiment". This brings about a margin of untranslatability which, paradoxically, is narrowed (or may be narrowed) in translations into other languages, but increases in width for the Italian reader who has not passed, with both attention and affection, through Verga and Pirandello. And it is partly for this reason that Brancati – indubitably the most interesting Italian writer of the 'Forties and 'Fifties – remains, in spite of inducements from the cinema, one of the least read and the worst read."

It is a novelty for a translator to find his text enjoying any advantage whatever over the original; but, though Sciascia makes a good point, we must beware of taking his words too much at face value. The question of "what it is to be Sicilian" is a constant undercurrent in Brancati's work, and a translator can do no more than hope that some of it emerges, even in English, of its own accord. Brancati, moreover, had what might be called a speciality: a peculiarity of the Sicilian male that has become known as *gallismo*, that feeling of being, or wishing to be – even in the vulgar sense of the word – cock of the roost with women, coupled in many case by an underlying self-distrust as well as all that is implied by the word *mamma*. A state of mind more complex than the "sexual conceit" which my excellent dictionary provides as a definition. *Gallismo* is not a feature of *The Lost Years*, but it comes into its own in the later *Don Giovanni in Sicilia* and (forthcoming from Harvill) *Il bell'Antonio*.

PATRICK CREAGH

PART ONE

I

ONE SEPTEMBER DAY Leonardo Barini left Rome, where he was editor of the literary magazine *Campoformio*, and went back to Natàca, a city on the Mediterranean and his birthplace.

In Rome he had been suffering from giddiness and dizzy spells: his health was in a bad way. But three weeks of rest and wholesome food in the bosom of his family would be enough to put him back on his feet. Obviously it couldn't be anything serious. Three weeks and he'd be off back to Rome.

Or so he said to himself as he pulled the bedclothes up over his eyes and his mother closed the shutters.

"Let me get forty winks, now."

His father, his mother, and his brother left the room, closing the door behind them . . . Dizzy spells? They'd soon pass. Three weeks and he'd be back in Rome . . .

But he wasn't as ill as all that, and the dizzy spells were not enough to explain away such a headlong homecoming. The truth was something else again, the truth was this: suddenly, for no apparent reason, Leonardo's heart had run out of joy. The lovely light which illumined everything, that gave meaning even to chairs and inkpots, had simply snuffed out. Ever since his earliest infancy this light had been with him, there in the cradle, there on his desk at school, it was everywhere always, and now it had gone. "Why?" Why had it gone? Without it he couldn't live; without it he was a numbskull, an incompetent, a paralytic fuddy-duddy.

A fig for dizziness and vomiting! Childish nonsense. But if

that light did not return, and the joy that had been in his heart for no reason, just as now it had left him for no reason, he would budge neither from that bed nor from his home. Others might without complaint live their whole lives long in such a gloom, but speaking for himself not another step could he take: he felt at death's door.

The telephone rang in the next room. He heard his mother's voice: "Yes, Leonardo's back, but he's sleeping."

"Mamma," he called out, "who is it?"

"The Careni girl, Lisa."

"Tell her I'm asleep."

"Yes, he's sleeping. Ring again in half an hour."

His mother's footsteps faded away along the dim corridor, past the antiquated armchairs and the occasional tables cluttered with figurines – St Antony with the Child in arms, St Rita in black cloak, St Peter, the man sick of the palsy at his side, and tiny red votive lights and withered flowers. Came a creak from the door of the box-room, there where piles of mattresses were kept for guests, along with the suitcases his father and mother had taken on their honeymoon, fruit of which was he himself, Leonardo. After which he heard nothing more except the almost imperceptible drip, drip, that had fallen year in year out into the water-butt in the courtyard.

Not fifteen minutes had passed in this manner before the telephone rang the second time.

"I don't know," said his mother. "I just don't know if he's awake yet."

"No, I'm not awake yet!" shouted Leonardo, who had still to shut an eye.

"Not yet, not yet," repeated his mother in her soft lilting voice. "He's still asleep."

The autumn leaves, borne on the warm wind, wafted right up to the balcony and shuffled to and fro outside the window like the footsteps of a stranger. Now and again a shutter banged; the autumn sirocco was blowing. At this time of day, Leonardo began to think, the sky will be oppressive, the pavements crammed with people wandering along, hands in pockets, opening their mouths before the mirroring shop windows, either to inspect their tongues or else, simply, to yawn. Avvocato De Marchi will be seated at a table in the *birreria* from which he will not stir until midnight, the cafés will be crammed, barracks-like, with men; the youngsters, in groups of ten or twenty, will have begun exchanging those shoves and pushes that send the skinny ones hurtling against the wall; on trestles in gas-lit suburbs long rows of fish will now be lying, chill as steel, and barefoot boys will surely be hurling insults at the diminutive, felt-hatted passers-by who have turned down those enormous, metallic fishes. Yes, this was the South. And the wind that banged the shutters came from Africa.

Leonardo turned over in bed. "That light of mine, why has it left me?" he thought. "Why has it forced me back down here? What has happened to my life? Nothing that could be called a crisis. Everything was going well when suddenly, darkness."

Again the telephone rang. "No," repeated his mother. "He's sleeping."

"Perhaps," Leonardo proceeded with his thoughts, his face so close to the wall as to catch a whiff of the old wallpaper, "perhaps it all comes from my illness and will clear up along with the dizzy spells and giddiness . . ." But he'd often been ill before, and far more seriously, and such a thing had never happened – that light had never gone out . . .

"No idea!" said his mother, back at the receiver. "No idea! He's resting."

. . . He hadn't been burning the candle at both ends, or committing any terrible sins; he hadn't been under any great strain either mental or physical, he had no particular worries. His life had been toddling along as ever. Why robbed of joy, then?

"Yes, still sleeping. Still asleep. He's resting."

This time he had no idea whether the words were his mother's on the telephone or his own mind churning them over. "He's resting! . . ." He wasn't resting one bit. A spasm of urgency had got into his head, and was milling around thus: "Three weeks and he'll have recovered! Three weeks and he'll be seeing everything in the same rosy hue that has always coloured it, that he wasn't even conscious of, so habitual and natural did it seem. Then he'll be off back to Rome, and leave the South and this city behind him as if it were a nasty black cloud dispersed by the wind. What he needs now is rest, plenty of rest . . ."

The leaves rustled on the balcony, the shutter banged back and forth in the African wind.

11

ON THE OTHER END of the line which Leonardo had refused to be summoned to, Signorina Lisa Careni was longing to impart a happy discovery she had made: how to spend the evening. She'd had this idea, snap!, just like that, while seated in a comfy chair reading a boring book. She had emitted the soft chirrup of a bird on seeing blue sky break through grey cloud, and rushed to the telephone to communicate her happy discovery to her girl-friends and boy-friends. The latter were few, for young females were not allowed boy-friends in Natàca.

A way to spend the evening, and indeed time in general, was a matter of vast importance in Natàca. After dusk the young men would stand around in groups mulling over where and how to spend the evening. Discussions would be interrupted by one of the group who, as if shaking himself free from some frightful dream and realizing that for an hour they had all been standing in front of the selfsame poster for a public auction, would come out with the stock phrase: "Well, who's dead here?"

Very common, in Natàca, this phrase. It meant that they'd been loafing on the same bit of pavement so long that in the centre of their circle there must be a corpse to identify.

On Saturdays the whole city was buzzing with discussion over where and how to spend Sunday. Even though many of the community either had jobs or were students, it nonetheless invariably happened that after working hours they found themselves with a great deal of free time to kill. For those who had nothing to do anyway, the situation was graver still. The latter were, for the most part, rich landowners, and alas, one of the first things with which wealth adorns a gilded youth is a watch, a large gold watch, a precise chronometer with four hands, one for the hours, one for the minutes, one for the seconds, and finally the slenderest of hands for the fractions of seconds. Hanging around outside the pastry cooks', these young fellows, with the merest twitch of the shirt-cuff, were able to measure their boredom to a T. They amused themselves by setting the stop-watch in motion when, say, their mutual friend Erasmo Veni, a well-known young man-about-town, whose spectacles bobbed about on a swarthy snout, started to sip at his cup of coffee. Erasmo deposited his empty cup on the counter exactly two hundred and three and two-fifths seconds later. In the same way it became common knowledge that the hand-kissing routine of Federico Reali, the most languid and elaborate of the scions of the nobility, lasted two seconds; that the kindly, cultured Signora Galli, before crossing the road, would dither on the kerb for fifty seconds; and that Carlo Dalbi propelled his spittle which – although he had sworn to spit no more and to become entirely the well-mannered young gent – escaped his lips in an unceasing stream at a speed of two metres per second, the equivalent of six kilometres an hour.

You can imagine that these calculations were not confined to superficialities. The speed of far more delicate and personal matters, at least in the case of the young men most in the public eye, was known to within a fair degree of accuracy. All the same, these many and various calculations never succeeded in occupying a whole hour at a time. The stop-watch hand scampered like a spider sighting a fly in her web, for a twinkling was still, then sprang into action again. But the other, the short, black, stubby one, never really took any serious steps to get a move on.

Apart from calculations to pass the time there were others to save it. Arriving home at night Carlo Dalbi would remove his left glove ten paces from the door and his right seven paces away. At a distance of five paces his gloves were already in his overcoat pocket, and when his hat brim touched the street door the key was there in his hand and to slip it into the lock was the work of a moment. Rodolfo De Mei, the young architect, always studious and retiring, but who had never achieved a thing in his life, now, out of the blue and for no apparent reason, began spouting phrases such as "We artists . . ." or "Speaking for myself, as an artist . . ." Even Rodolfo De Mei tried to save time by reading, at mealtimes, vast architectural periodicals which dismally overshadowed his younger brother's plate.

But even these efforts to save time concealed the desire to speed it on. There were hours at Natàca so sluggish that they would not budge for love nor money. However, some way of getting round them was always found. Subtle wits were at work! The rub was that, once past, those hours left nothing to be remembered, not even weariness from the exertion of so laboriously shoving them along. They bore an uncanny resemblance to one another, so that many evenings were remembered as one, and a stream of Sundays as scarcely a single day.

Yes, the thought of the future was burdensome, but that of the past not so in the least. The impression of having woken up in old age after a week or two of youth was one of the commonest among the old men of Natàca. From this sprang their air of unfulfilment, their brash gay-old-doggery, their distressing mania for amorous sallies. The "Coronets Club", frequented solely by elderly men, when the cane chairs were set out on the pavement in springtime became a veritable ogres' lair of a place. The girls, who passed by practically at a run, would hear the club reverberate with sepulchral enticements, the smack of lips kissing the empty air, and the rasp of chairs pushed heavily back by those of a mind to rise and pursue the gamebirds.

If the old men were so little resigned to their fate, the youngsters were positively soured. It was all, according to Ninì Padeni, ex-lieutenant in the Bersaglieri, and a fine, tall, lean young figure of a man, who used to amaze the ladies of the "Pensione Orange Blossom" by mounting on the tables and poking his head between his legs, it was all due to the "brutal separation of the sexes" under which the city had lived for centuries. According to others, it was all due to the heat, to the sirocco . . . No one, in fact, had the ghost of a notion what "it" was all due to. But it's a fact that, what with people sauntering up and down the same stretch of pavement for hours on end, occasionally making vague gestures of impatience though in reality expecting no one, and others who hung around hours on end listening to a tune they didn't care for at all, it was the stray dogs, with their undeviating course, their air of having an aim and a purpose (people wondered with a touch of envy where on earth the dogs were going), who alone kept the prestige of Western culture flying at the masthead.

When the telephone rang again and Leonardo made up his mind to answer it, Lisa Careni spoke as follows:

"I'd thought up a really lovely way of spending a whole half-day. But unfortunately it's not allowed. For the afternoon there's a solution: giving my cousin a dancing-lesson. But what about this evening?"

"Don't know." This from Leonardo. "I really don't."

"Even you haven't an inkling?"

"Not a one."

"Doesn't matter. We'll expect you tomorrow evening all the same. Come just as you are, without an inkling!"

"All right," mumbled Leonardo, and crawled back to bed.

III

THE TWIN LIVING-ROOMS at the Careni's were jam-packed with young people. Dora, the sleepy old Alsatian, lumbered about among their legs with half-closed eyes, wagging her tail and sniffing at everyone's shoes. She was a funny-looking dog, with a face verging on the pensive, to which her wrinkly, droopy eye-lids lent an air of severity. Nothing would ever satisfy her, not the siesta-time silence in the house, broken only by her sharp, nervous barks, not the children's hullabaloo nor the racket of the younger set, not Lisa's singing nor her elder sister Maria's efforts on the piano. She responded languidly, with apparent indifference, to the reproaches of Lisa whom she was, as they say, mad about, gazing at her with those great eyes in which something akin to a patch of oil was forever swimming. Company, when it arrived, provided her with some momentary relief and jollity. Dora leapt to sniff the shoes of the first comer, passing on to those of the second, the third, the fourth, and fifth, but she very soon got disheartened and curled up again, as if she had been on an age-long search for someone, and even now had failed to find him. A minute or two later she would rise shakily to her feet once more and set off to sniff the shoes of the fifth, the fourth, the third, the second, and the first-comer, but this time more deliberately, with the air of one going back to rummage in a drawer already ransacked in vain. Three times she would repeat this exploratory perambulation, and then doze off with her head on her paws, breathing lethargically through her wrinkly nostrils. Frightful dreams! Now and again she tried to wake up, it seemed; but she couldn't make it.

"What's up with that dog?" asked Leonardo.

"Leave the dog out of it," retorted Lisa. "What I want to know is why you've come back from Rome so all of a sudden. How *can* anyone leave Rome?"

"I haven't left for ever . . . I'm going back."

"Soon?"

"Just as soon as I've recovered."

"And when do you think that'll be?"

"In three weeks."

"Three weeks, eh? Seems a bit long. Mind you, I'm very glad to see you here in our midst, but I've always thought that a young man like you goes all to pieces down here, and ends up as a wet rag."

"How right you are! But I'll be off soon. After all, I'm not *that* ill."

A grey mist thereupon descended before his eyes, and the chandelier seemed about to flicker out. After leaving home that morning he had seen the long stretch of the Corso dance like an island viewed from a small boat in a choppy sea; the backs of the passers-by, clad almost every one in dark cloth, gave the place an unbearable ants'-nest look; his knees trembled and sharp stabs of cold smote him on the shoulders, as if his jacket were coming unstitched and leaving them bare to the winds. At times it seemed to him that everything was being inexorably crushed earthwards and passers-by must soon be spread out on the ground like carpets. He had tried to put up a fight against this weight, the sole result being a stagger to one side or the other. A swarm of flies hovered in the air, along with other twisty creatures much like the little hairs that fly from a barber's scissors. Look, even at this moment, in the lamplight one of those wisps is floating, ever on its way floorwards . . .

"Come on Leo, cheer up!"

"Why? Do I seem in the dumps?"

"You're thinking too much . . . Oh goody goody your friends have arrived."

Rodolfo De Mei and Giovanni Luisi had that moment appeared in the doorway. Like Leonardo they had recently returned from Rome for a short stay in Natàca, and were always on the point of redeparture.

Great fuss was made of Leonardo, with plenty of hefty back-slapping and affectionate taunts such as "Here he is, the pest! . . . All we needed was another nitwit! . . . Off again soon, we hope!"

"Why do you tease him so?" asked Signora Careni with kindly astonishment. "He's your friend!"

"Friend?" cried Giovanni. "We're brothers!"

"Ah, I thought as much. And tomorrow, the three of you . . . By the way, Giovanni, I suppose there's no truth in the rumour that you mean to stay on here for ever?"

"For ever?" Giovanni burst out laughing, and went on laughing a goodish while after his mouth might have preferred to take a rest. "It'll be a miracle if I stay till next Saturday. Who are these witches who want to bury us down here?"

"How can you say such a thing? I believe I heard it from your mother."

"Our mothers are our worst enemies," put in Rodolfo De Mei. "The Sicilian *mamma* who brings us into the world only to gobble us up."

"Rodolfo!" shrieked Signora Careni. "You can't say things like that to a mother! Good Lord, what a rude boy you are!"

"But you *know* it's true. For ten years now, that is, ever since I took to going out of an evening, my mother has been saying 'Rodolfo, think of your poor mother, don't come home late.' And I've always replied, 'Of course not, mum.' Ten years of 'Rodolfo, think of your poor mother, don't be home late,' and 'Of course not, mum,' well, it makes you think! All the same, my mother's fondest wish is for this to go on for another thirty years."

"Naturally, poor woman!"

"Yes, yes of course, poor woman, yes . . . But I still sleep in the night-nursery; every morning our maid brings me coffee and treats me just the same as fifteen years ago. And why should she treat me differently, since even this morning, before she came into my room, she heard my mother say, 'Do look and see if the children are awake yet.' One of these children is *me*. And the other is my younger brother who is twenty-five."

"And isn't all this very sweet of her?" asked Signora Careni.

"Sweet it may be, in fact very sweet indeed. But I can't help feeling that if I want to be a man I have to get out of here."

"Why should the maternal nest ever change?" broke in Giovanni. "The maternal nest is incapable of change, since not a thing has changed within it. Basically it's stayed exactly as it was. It's fifteen years since you were twelve, but what of it? It's still a household with a dad and a mum and two kids."

"But the children are grown men now!"

"Is *that* any reason for their mamas to stop loving them?"

"By all means let her love them, but let her also respect them as grown men, give them a chance to leave home, not expect always to have her eye on them as if they were toddlers as likely to tumble over as to stand up. If need be, not to mince words – let her love 'em a bit less."

"But you're saying the most frightful things," protested Signora Careni.

"Frightful or not, it's the truth. The truth is that at twenty-eight a man can't go on living in the same house as 'mum and dad' without looking silly."

"Stuff and nonsense," exclaimed Giovanni. "In Natàca, as a bachelor, I wouldn't know how to live anywhere but the house where I was born. It does my heart good at hear my father passing my door in the morning and bawling at all and sundry to pipe down so as not to wake me. The very bellow which has always woken me up, and always given me a chuckle. Same goes for my mother bringing in my coffee and eyeing my cosy little bed, always wondering should she pop another blanket on."

"And don't *you* think it's silly for a man of thirty to say 'my cosy little bed'?"

"Yes, yes, silly as you like . . . By Jove, that's a splendid picture!"

It must be said at this point that Giovanni Luisi was given to such volatile fits and starts. His attention was apt to skip, like a bird alighting here, there and everywhere, but at the least sound taking wing and vanishing.

"What a splendid little picture! Who did it?"

"A young barber," said Lisa. "He really is awfully good."

"Aha, a barber! . . . These barbers are never just plain and simple barbers, are they?"

"You're really going in for profound observations this evening," said Rodolfo with a touch of malevolence. "Give us your thoughts on tailors then. Or cobblers. Your cobblers, now, they'd repay a bit of study."

"Well, what else would you like to talk about?"

"Actually, in point of fact, there *was* a subject under discussion," broke in Avvocato Paolo Filesi who, silent throughout this conversation, had been squeezing the last drops of tea from the slice of lemon stranded at the bottom of his cup, and occasionally fingering the exaggeratedly high silk collar within which his head swivelled, now to left and now to right, like a very aloof slow-motion lighthouse. This young solicitor was very social: wherever he looked he saw drawing-rooms and demoiselles, he called Lisa Careni "Donna Lisa". Confronted with a cup of tea, either he maintained an inscrutable silence during which he saw glittering, modish visions rise from the cup, the forms of women with veiled glances, extending a bare arm culminating in a drooping hand to be kissed, or else he was seized by a positive paroxysm of eloquence, and with many a "don't you know" and "agreed?" led the conversation round to a point which he would have mistaken for a conclusion had not someone else taken the liberty of observing, "But this is where we came in!"

"Actually, in point of fact, there *was* a subject under discussion," insisted the solicitor. "Actually it was the question of living at home with our parents."

"Oh, yes, ha ha," snorted Giovanni. "Some life! Positively mummified!"

And here we should further add that Giovanni Luisi never stuck to his own opinion about any matter for more than two minutes on end. The ability to say of an identical thing that it was beautiful, hideous, amusing, tedious, black, or white, was his true forte. According to Rodolfo De Mei, fate had blundered in not providing Giovanni with two separate mouths, one of which could be saying "You genius, you!" precisely while the other was saying "You moron!"

"Thanks be to God," muttered Rodolfo. "You've finally come round to my opinion."

"Naturally. How could anyone think it's any fun to live in this place? Good Lord! . . . On the other hand, if anyone wants to live here let them get on with it. We're not interested. I'm off next week, you in a month . . ."

"And what about you, Leonardo?" asked Maria Careni.

"Er, me? In three weeks . . ."

"Lucky old you!" murmured Lisa. "To get away – what heaven! But mind you, there's no knowing," and the girl's eyes sparkled as if over a glass raised in a toast, "there's no knowing whether *we* may not be leaving too!"

"I could wish nothing better for you, Donna Lisa," intoned the solicitor, raising her hand, kissing it, replacing it on her lap and giving it a little pat. "I could wish nothing better."

The dog Dora lumbered to her feet to sniff at everyone's shoes again. She moved heavily, like someone who has dozed off in a café and now at the waiter's suggestion is making his way glassy-eyed to the cloakroom in search of his overcoat among the many.

"Ladies and gentlemen," cried Maria, in great excitement, "it's already after . . . guess what time!"

"Ten o'clock?"

"Eleven!" cried the girl jubilantly. "Eleven o'clock! We've got through the evening. I just can't imagine how it passed so quickly!"

"Let's be off, then," said the solicitor. "If we've got it over with, let's be off." In so saying he had risen to his feet, checking an urge to stretch and yawn – a rare and deplorable impulse in arms and torso habitually schooled to such decorum.

IV

NOT ONCE BUT TWICE had those "three weeks" passed, and Leonardo was still around. His health was on the mend but something else, much more important than health, was utterly stationary. The citizens of Natàca had too much spare time to ignore such a nice problem as that of an individual who stays in Natàca week after week even though he has a job in Rome. Friends, acquaintances, a copious body of strangers, including friends of his brother's, his father's, and people who imagined they knew Leonardo simply because they were at the photographer's when he happened to pop in, or others who had, like him, spent months in Rome; or who, standing at the telegram counter, had muttered "Do they call this service?" at the very moment Leonardo said "This service is a disgrace!" – all these, smiling with a hint of reproof, asked Leonardo, "Not off yet?"

"In a day or two," replied he, smiling apologetically back.

"Not three weeks any more, eh?"

"No, not any longer."

But no sooner did he think of the train, of Rome, and of Roman cooking, than he felt that someone was out to strip his living flesh of one of the mainstays of life, something indispensable to staying on his feet, eating, drinking, sleeping. Then he would say to himself, as if to exorcize this mysterious someone, "No, I'll hang on. I won't leave so soon. I'll hang on."

Besides, Giovanni Luisi also was postponing his departure

for Rome. His mother had informed him that it was going to be a cold winter; in the middle of his bedroom floor she had set a pan of charcoal embers which, in addition to the warmth, gave forth a scent of the woods recalling the days of his childhood and consequently the fear of separation from mamma; she had presented him with large sums of money for the purchase of Russian novels; she had inveigled him into wearing woollen knee-warmers and a thick vest; she had bought him a radiogram and several of the latest records; and finally she had promised to stop opening his post, or, at any rate, to refrain in future from burning certain letters from women unless he had seen them first.

During the long afternoons, stretched on his bed and swathed in a shawl, while the Russian novel held in a hand poking half out from under like a little claw instructed him that life is a pretty serious business, and the wind, entering through the worm-eaten shutters, fanned up the embers in the brazier, Giovanni began to feel there was no chance that winter of removing the knee-warmers, the flannel cummerbund, the thick vest and the woollen drawers cross-laced at the calves. He ought not to have given way to his mother but, once having done so, he would have to wait until spring to get back into a slimmer and more dignified outfit. And since the idea of living in Rome, to be attractive, had to involve the idea of a girl, and as the thought of a girl did not really fit with the thought of those long johns, that flannel cummerbund, those knee-warmers concealed beneath his suit, the whole thing boiled down to the fact that the very idea of leaving Natàca must be postponed until the spring.

Anyway, it was no fun, life in Rome, hanging about in the anterooms of ministers and generals, stared down at by those gloomy seventeenth-century paintings, with the footsteps of the usher passing to and fro, and every couple of hours the ringing of the bell that wrenched some minuscule figure from a chair which had all but engulfed him. It was no fun, no fun at all! If the general wished to help Giovanni, and at last procure him a salaried post, he could easily give him that helping hand in the spring and give it, what's more, from afar.

Rodolfo De Mei, on the contrary, was a spirited young fellow, and on the point of locking his suitcases when a telephone call from his uncle, a professor in the university, apprised him that a certain mansion in a most salubrious neighbourhood was about to disgorge a Client. The client in question was Duke Fausto Villadora, by no means a negligible personage, the possessor of more orchards and vineyards, farmsteads and palm-groves than he knew of himself. These orchards were, however, abandoned, and if it is true that lands thrive in the light of the owner's eye, his must have been as dry as a bone. For years now the owner's eye had viewed neither meadow nor mansion, but had remained riveted upon the mirror, scrutinizing the face to which it belonged. Was not the brow too pallid, the nose perhaps too peaky? For a long time this affluent gentleman had been taking every precaution against death with such diligence and solicitude as to rob himself of both sleep and appetite. Not that he was ill. But need one really be *ill*, to die? And then, show me the man who is completely sound. Microbes come thronging in on every side, there are millions, billions of them; nothing on earth that isn't swarming with microbes. They are silent, invisible, but this affluent gentleman could no longer be sure that he didn't both see and hear them. By night he heard them seething on his pillow and over the bedclothes, he heard them softly humming about the peachstone left lying on the bedside table. As for seeing them, frankly, he didn't; but now and again something came flickering round his mouth and, wherever he was, be it in café or theatre, he would huff and would puff till he blew away those millions of tiny mites set on his death.

Needless to say he did not devote the same care to defending his properties. How could he? Where could he find the time? A conscientious man defends either his person or his properties. He maintained, and perhaps not mistakenly, that his blue blood was a greater asset than the water to irrigate his orchards, and the bronchi of his lungs of more exquisite concern than the branches of his orange-trees. So it was that each year the drought in the dry streambeds laid low many a citrus tree, his estates were gateless, wall-less, pathless, his houses sprouted mould like grottoes, his cattle became tubercular, his stewards fleeced him; but by way of compensation everything in the master's body was as regular as clockwork and read like an open book. Every morning he assessed the state of his bladder, his blood pressure, his pulse rate, his body-weight; his drinking water was sterilized, his food weighed out and thoroughly cooked; getting dressed was an occasion for very ingenious precautions, such as pulling his shirt on from the feet up, so that the indubitably unsterilized fabric should not pass right over his nose and mouth. In recent years, however, the tedium of always taking the same precautions against – hush, let us whisper it – death, inventor of all sorts of tricks for insinuating its microbes into the human body (allied to the truly discomforting thought that in the end, one way or another, death was bound to win), and the stale air in his room, and a certain friend of his who had offered sound advice, and the unaccustomed sense of wellbeing he had gained from the sight of a robin perched on the balcony railing, as if God looked kindly upon those who don't have death on the brain . . . in short, a whole assemblage of circumstances had induced him to take more interest in his lands and houses. The idea of a monumental entrance gate to his estates at P. diverted him.

That certain friend, who was also a friend of Professor Avellino, Rodolfo's uncle, had recommended a young architect, an up-and-coming talent, "a lad who'll do you a good job."

For ten days Rodolfo was on the *qui vive* for his affluent client. The maid had orders to show him into the red sitting-room, and it was the devil of a job to make her promise to say to the visitor, "The *signor architetto* will be informed immediately of your arrival."

"But why?" she kept on asking. "If the gentleman has come

looking for Master Mimì, why should I announce him to this *signor architetto?*"

"You'll do as you're told!" shrieked the lady of the house.

Meanwhile the client was long in coming, and more than once Rodolfo found himself cursing the day he had unpacked his cases.

At long last, one afternoon, the duke crossed the De Mei threshold. He had no colour in his cheeks and no wish to deposit in the hallway either his overcoat or his scarf, which he persisted in using as a filter between his own mouth and that of his interlocutor. Rodolfo, eager to give this precious personage a warm welcome, was forced to be content with shaking two frigid fingers, instantly withdrawn.

"At your service," said Rodolfo, seating himself on a hard chair. But the affluent gentleman was scanning the tiled floor with a listless yet wary eye.

"How can I help you?" prompted Rodolfo.

"Do you," said the duke almost in a whisper, "make a habit of spitting on the floor in this place?"

Rodolfo turned puce, and his first impulse was to pull that detestable scarf tight, make a leash of it, haul the affluent gentleman through room after room to the top of the stairs, and kick him down them. But he checked himself.

"Indeed not!" he replied. "I cannot imagine what suggested such an idea."

"Those drops down there? . . ."

"Merely a spot of water from the flower-vase."

"Ah, I beg your pardon."

The affluent gentleman then gave laborious expression to his wish for a monumental gateway to his estates at P.; Rodolfo effusively vowed that he would do his utmost; there followed a moment of embarrassed silence during which neither could find anything to say; and then the gentleman, peering suspiciously here and there, withdrew from the De Mei household.

Ten days later, when Rodolfo presented his client with the tinted drawing of a gateway consisting of two enormously high blank walls connected by a low, mean entrance, the gentleman pulled a whole gamut of faces, broke into a fit of coughing, and finally, rising, pronounced a few words which, reported shortly afterwards by Rodolfo to his mother, father and brother, were explained, clarified and rounded off as if the gentleman had said, "Good, we shall discuss this again in a month's time, meanwhile I'll also give you something else to think about!" That "good," as well as the word "also", were part of the supplement entirely invented to make the client's phrase sound serious and plausible.

In a sudden tantrum Rodolfo threw everything that came to hand higgledy-piggledy into his suitcases; but even as his cases swelled the more clearly he remembered having spent the money intended for the journey and the early days in Rome on the acquisition of shelves and armchairs for the Red Sitting-Room. This, also, at his mother's suggestion. That little woman was tougher and craftier than he'd ever imagined. In a word, she was the winner: he was obliged to stay in Natàca. But for how long? That was the point – for how long? When spring came, even at the cost of clinging to a swallow's tail, would he not take flight?

However, neither he nor Giovanni did leave. Leonardo therefore was provided with two "travelling companions" who had suffered the same mishap as himself – to be bogged down in Natàca, waiting for the train of life, which erstwhile had made good speed but now had juddered to a halt, to pick up steam for Rome.

V

Leonardo woke early but lay about for ages listening to the stream of passing costermongers hawking "Lettuces tender as water!" and "Prickly-pears finer than ice-cream!" and vociferously enquiring of their own apples, "How, O how can you dare to be so sweet?"

Prone in bed in the dark is the most felicitous position for killing time, now letting your eyes close, now lending an ear to the street noises, now to the flies hunting daylight at the crack between the shutters; sometimes nodding off, at others thinking thoughts that could easily be the hem of a dream, you slip from eight to eleven – hey presto! – in a jiffy.

At eleven Leonardo rose from his bed, washed, breakfasted, dressed and, before going out, rested his brow for a while against the window-pane and took in the little piazza below. Oh! these piazzas where nothing ever happens! How is it that nothing ever happens? Let's take a look . . . try to fathom how it is that nothing ever happens. It's a fascinating show, forever new and ultimately inexplicable, this life which never gives birth to a damn thing.

"What a bunch!" muttered Leonardo. "Absolute Arabs!"

He left the house at half-past twelve. The only street in Natàca with any life in it was the long, straight Corso, all dark paving stones and dark, pot-bellied baroque *palazzi*. The sun beat first on one pavement then on the other, and from one side to the other people passed with the sun. All walked at a snail's pace, poising each foot for as long as possible in air. It was unavailing indeed, and perhaps even blameworthy, to walk fast, for you no sooner fetched up at one end of the Corso than you had to turn round and fetch up at the other, then down again, and up again, and down again, and up again, so many, many times, that either you could no longer count them or else were afraid to.

Almost everyone knew each other, and almost everyone exchanged greetings, at first with genial effusive nods, then with nods of a brusquer sort, then, when the renewed "good-mornings" began to take on a mocking ring, and the very sight of each other what a barred window means to a convict, they greeted each other no longer, but mutually began to desire the other's instant removal or, on occasion, death.

No one bothered to keep his voice down, so the air was vibrant with phrases such as, "I said to her, either you're no better than you ought to be, or you're just a poor mutt! . . . First night I was married I went off to a hotel, and when she . . ." The men of law would greet one another from a distance, each declaring himself to be the other's humble servant, each eager to kiss the other's hand, to be at his service. Whenever a pretty girl went by, escorted by mother, the lads would wink at each other, and a whole gang of them would totter and sway as though before an invisible charge by mounted police. The girls had laughter in their hearts, but their mouths affected disdain, and eventually their hearts too ceased to laugh, because none of those gangs of lads ever came up with a husband for them. "They do nothing but loaf around," said the girls to one another. "They don't take anything seriously and are just spiteful beasts without a good word to say for anything. Motes they see in our eyes but devil a beam in their sisters'!"

In point of fact the lads were not looking at the girls for their motes, but for things as unmotelike as you can well imagine, and they gave vent to genuine outbursts of glee and appreciation. Very susceptible they were to female charms, but unlike their fathers and grandfathers before them they expressed no wish to put themselves heart and soul into the business, to stake therein their lives and peace of mind. In a word, they had no wish to risk killing themselves for love or anyone else from jealousy. By constantly guarding against this risk they had become a bunch of bears, unable even to talk to girls without giving offence. When a friend came back home from the North with a wife from those parts, the boys were truly hard pressed: asked round to supper they'd talk all the time to their host, never a word to his wife. And later on, when their hostess moved to the piano, they didn't know where to look, how to sit still, or where to put their hands, while in their minds they mulled over the compliments they would pay – but never did pay – when the piece ended.

The young ladies of Natàca understood all, and despised it. An indefinable antagonism had therefore sprung up between the girls and the boys, on whom the former but rarely bestowed a smile. Only on certain rainy evenings, when a party going in one direction had to hoist umbrellas to yield to a party coming in the other, forming for an instant little silk-canopied pavilions, if in one of these fleeting pavilions there happened to be a young man and a maid, and she gave him a look that at the time seemed like any other look, but two hours later, back home, the young man found that he still had that look in the marrow of his bones . . . ah then it was unwilling to let him sleep. It hankered to tell him, one by one, of all the evenings that girl had spent housebound, her forehead pressed against the window-pane, and of all the small illusions, all the fond hopes, all the small loves nipped in the bud. The telling of it ceased only at daybreak, and only at daybreak did the young man fall into a sleep soured with pangs of conscience.

VI

AFTER LUNCH LEONARDO relaxed in an armchair, feet on another chair, legs swathed in shawls. The shutters were wide open and the panes a-glitter with distant objects, other little windows through which came a frequent glimpse of a dancing figure, for the buildings in Natàca had no heating and, mild though the winter was, hands and feet turned to stone some afternoons and people would often leap up and skip about until the blood came back into their fingertips.

Leonardo opened a book, had a go at it, but whatever was in it was as nothing compared with the thoughts that hours spent with books had once been full of delight and life, whereas now they were a dead bore. What hand had reduced all the world's best books to childish frivolities? Even in the great masterpieces he now found a touch of dullness, futility, shabbiness.

His eyes strayed from the page towards the rooftops where pigeons were strutting, very slowly because it was already evening, and it seems that pigeons pay homage to the gloaming, to windows lighting up and stars above the rooftops.

Leonardo stood up numb with cold, flapped his arms two or three times, put on his overcoat and left the house.

Light from the streetlamps made the paving-stones the darker, light fled in the face of the dark that exuded from the earth, the walls, the black-clad crowd – a male every one of them, and with dragging footsteps . . .

The cafés too were packed with men, many of whom would certainly be sitting there far into the night, all cheery at first, but thereafter gloomy and woebegone, as if mysteriously manacled together beneath the tables. The men standing under the red glare of the illuminated signs caught it full in the face, and the look it gave them was frenzied, almost diabolical.

On the doorstep of the best pastrycook's in town young Rosso Autini was making a problem of everything and providing brilliant answers for all to hear. He discoursed upon the new officers' uniform, the way to parry a sabre-cut to the body, the music of Verdi, the latest film, the use of traffic lights. Any interruptor was met with such comments as "Roberto, you are contemptible!" or "You, Francesco, have grasped my concept." At the height of his oratory and pleased as Punch with himself, to stay his fall into total self-adulation, he did a few tricks with his thumb, swooping it this way and that and going *buzz buzz*. Rodolfo De Mei, big feet planted wide apart and a well-bred smile on his lips, was prepared to listen to anything, to give every sign of good nature and if possible to embody it. Now and again he frowned, and the groove in his brow expressed his primary concern: not to allow the murky turmoil within him to boil down to the simple question, "What depths have I sunk to?" A spirited young fellow was Rodolfo, who wanted life to be fun, busy and satisfying, and he kept a constant eye on it so that everywhere, even in Natàca, it would continue to be satisfying, busy and fun.

Giovanni Luisi played along with the tricks, clumsily attempting to ape Autini and seeming in his seventh heaven, when all of a sudden he scowled and muttered that nothing could be more awful than what was going on before his eyes, and he conniving with it. Then he came over all merry again, thinking he would soon be off to Rome. Then he thought he'd never go there again. Then that perhaps he would. And in the end he had not a thought in his head except that it was late and at all costs he must be getting back to dinner.

He was seen to his front door by Leonardo, Rodolfo and Paolo Filesi, the skinny solicitor. As they passed the "Robertoni" Pharmacy some noteworthy persons were to be seen grouped outside. These included Professor Neri, an old buffer in a yellow overcoat scarcely longer than his jacket, the inventor of Morreale, a new universal language which consisted in discovering the roots or – as he expressed it – the "radicals" of a word (from Lat. *radix* root, *radus* being however a dissimilated form of *rarus* rare + X for the Unknown, the meaning of the whole being "rare mystery", i.e. "all clear"). He was always short of cash because his children had had him deprived of legal rights. Then there was old Leopoldi, a student of perpetual motion (also in need of funds), a number of dialect poets, Nereggia the author of sacred dramas in blank verse, and Avvocato De Marchi, composer of music. They formed no less than an academy in miniature, but from their attentions the four friends were anxious to escape, because they were strapped for cash and had no wish, at their age, to beg another penny from their mothers before midnight.

Around these personages, all well known in town and all markedly spiritual in appearance, hovered certain others, a harum-scarum crew, either playing or plotting some mean trick, gathering like jackals wherever they could sniff out some grey-matter that had gone a bit off, getting their fangs into any citizen who revealed some trifling mania or faint propensity to madness, and subjecting him to so many and various pranks, trials and tribulations that one fine day the poor devil would cry out that he could fly, and try to launch himself from a window in order, he claimed, to soar aloft.

The ringleader of this gang, Nello Tommasini, was able through his flourishing russet moustache to produce the most engaging smile in town. He swiftly made himself indispensable to his victims, who eventually preferred his deadly monkey-tricks to the most loving solicitudes of their nearest and dearest.

Tommasini responded to the greetings of the four friends with ample gestures, smiling affably and, from long-established professional habit, watching them out of the corner of his eye in case one of them was developing some minor crankiness to be borne in mind.

After dinner the friends met up again in the Luisi dining-room. The room was large, the floor covered with a jigsaw of overlapping carpets, the whole cluttered with furniture, chairs comfy and otherwise, sofas, tables, pictures, statuettes, laden dishes, plus a wood fire and a radiogram. Inset in one wall were two glass showcases, big as shop windows, displaying pyramids of porcelain, out-moded coffee-services, glasses of every shape and size. Above this display two plaster angels gazed down as they plucked petals from a garland. In the centre of the painted ceiling a buxom female bared her bosom and seemed on the point of casting one of her rotundities down upon the dining-table. Until the end of January the dishes on the sideboard were heaped with grapes, then were turned over to pears, oranges, apples, prunes black as olives and olives big as prunes.

Shortly after nine the worthy Signora Luisi rose from the table, wished her son good-night with a kiss on the forehead and a fondle to the nape of the neck and – with cajolements such as "Now, my lamb, you won't be going out this evening, *will* you dear boy" – took herself off to bed. Dr Luisi, stubbing out his pipe with a thumb, got to his feet in turn and with an affectionate "So long, you bunch of scallywags," left the room.

With the young people remained Giovanni's uncle, Roberto, who worked at the Customs and Excise, a chubby, rosy-cheeked, cheerful fellow, always glad it was others doing the talking rather than himself, and content that they were saying whatever they were saying. He'd had some rum times when he was young, traces of which survived in a local rag where numerous articles had appeared under his name, some of them even quite intelligent. He wrote no longer, and seldom spoke, but his ruddy complexion and glittering eyes proclaimed that for some years now something exceedingly pleasant had been taking place inside him – something it was as well to keep dark about. The four friends started on their heart-to-hearts in his presence, but he was an odd sort of audience, as if he were nodding off happily over some variety number.

"Lads," he would say eventually, "I have to work tomorrow. I bid you good-night. I'm off." And he too departed the dining-room.

"He's a moron," murmured Giovanni.

Alone at last they switched on the wireless and filled the room with the strains of light music. Radio Toulouse, Radio Budapest, bringing you the cafés of Toulouse, of Budapest, the racket of drums and saxophones, chinking of china, clinking of glasses, tinkling laughter of women.

Avvocato Paolo Filesi drifted into daydreams. Head relaxed on the back of the sofa, his gaze fixed on the painted figure on the ceiling, he announced that a gypsy-woman had foretold he would soon be a rich man, and said how "nice" it would be in Rome by night, walking home the girl who had been with him for hours in his bedroom . . . with that chill in the air, that little hand in his.

Rodolfo said that life without money was perfectly futile. Art? OK. Work? OK. But not in Natàca and never if you're moneyless. O to live in one of those bijou modern homes one sees in American movies, with a nice little staircase leading up to the bedrooms and there at the top a girl in a dressing-gown cooing "Rodolfo darling!" . . .

Leonardo continued to think that everything had once been bright and delightful, and now was all ugly and horrid. Really as if someone had taken all the light out of things. When O when would it be restored? Only then would he be capable of making a move towards Rome. How could he possibly go off at this juncture, how could he travel that far with this darkness gripping him at heart?

Thereafter the conversation took a turn towards banality: oughtn't they to get married? Certainly, but who to?

Giovanni expressed a terror of the night when he'd wake up at his wife's side, and she asleep and breathing softly under the blankets, and he would be struck by the thought – "My God, I don't fancy this one any more, and no power on earth can turn her out of my bed!"

"But why shouldn't you fancy her any more?" asked Paolo.

"Don't ask me. All I know is that I've never fancied any girl for more than a month. Even the prettiest, even the sweetest of them, after a month they come over all strange, and give you such funny looks that you can't help getting fed up with them."

"Well, with a millstone like that, you're certainly not likely to get married."

"Nonsense! I *want* to get married. It's just not the right moment yet, that's all."

And although he was past thirty his thoughts turned to Mummy and Daddy, and he knew that for a few years to come, though he didn't quite know why or what for, he would still need them. Maybe another year, maybe two . . .

Paolo, for his part, had every intention of marrying just as soon as he was rich. Rodolfo shared this view. Leonardo would marry when the light came back.

In fact these fellows, though shy, were immensely fond of children. They were given to chucking them under the chin in the park, while pretending to be roguishly making up to their nursemaids. A pair of eyes gazing up at them out of a face so familiar to each one from all those portraits and likenesses, and certain quirks and mannerisms, tricks of speech or tilts of the head (things in their own persons long since jaded and tiresome), for these to spring to life in the world again, once more amusing and graceful – to have children of their own, in short – would have been a true gift of God to these young men.

But how can a man marry when his life is so full of loose ends?

"That's enough boredom for the time being," said Rodolfo out of the blue. "Let's get home."

Christmas. Over the wireless come the chimes of the church-bells of Bethlehem. The plates, the glasses, the carafes, the fruit-bowls, the chandelier – all is a-tremble with that *carillon*. Giovanni switches off the lights.

When, after a moment or two, he puts them on again, it is as if the four friends have had a long, refreshing sleep, after which there is reason to hope that life will be more lively and more gladsome.

"The others'll soon be off back to Rome," says Rodolfo to himself, tossing back the last few drops in his glass.

VII

MEANWHILE THE WINTER had to be got through or, as in Natàca the saying was, killed off. Trips up the Mountain were organized (the one great mountain on the whole coast, and very high it was: snow-covered from head to foot, in the midst of a green countryside, it suggested a polar bear stranded in a Mediterranean meadow), and excursions to Turrenia, a small town consisting of hotels, guest-houses and gardens, and populated almost entirely by foreigners. Lello Raveni contributed his handsome automobile, the friends paid the petrol.

These jaunts to Turrenia always began with high hopes. In the lounge of the Grand Hotel the five chums sat around a small table laughing and drinking tea. The dance-band played away, the view from the picture-window was half sky and half sea. And what a sea! "Be-yoo-tiful!" exclaimed the foreign ladies at the neighbouring table.

Lello withdrew little by little into his own thoughts, silent as an empty sack. He was in love with the family's housemaid, and the toes of the shoes he left out to be polished were stuffed with impassioned letters. But his father had his suspicions (maybe he fancied the girl himself), and threatened every morning to turn the lot of them out of house and home. These thoughts plunged Lello into bitter torment, causing him to pluck gently at his sketch of a blond moustache.

"Lello, for goodness' sake stop that!" exploded Rodolfo, pushing the other's hand aside.

"Oh, quite," murmured Lello, coming to the surface. But

in no time his cheek sank back onto his closed fist, the fist opened, and the fingers again began to pluck . . .

But which of the five had not yet fallen to daydreaming? Those foreign ladies, so relaxed, with their evident hygiene of the mind announcing that no desire had ever been allowed to fester in their bosoms, in those bodies laved by Pacific and Atlantic, were like swallows alighting at a prisoner's window. Asking them to dance was obviously not on, just as no prisoner thinks of clutching at a swallow. Avvocato Filesi was alone in crossing the room, fingering his high silk collar. He made his bow, spoke a word, heard another in return, straightened up, and slow, dignified and scarlet in the face, regained his chair.

"She doesn't dance," he sighed.

The return journey they made late in the evening. From the back seat Leonardo scanned the heads of his two friends in front, those two well-beloved bubbles flying along between the black, star-studded windows, flying along so full of hopes and desires. With Rodolfo's skinny arm on this side and Giovanni's brawny one on the other, in some strange way he was heartened by the warmth of the two bodies, and mumbled a sort of prayer: that the lost lamp should return to the world, the light be restored to things, the joy and the fortitude to his heart; that his lips should spout words of cheer and encouragement to those good fellows around him . . . The evenings they came back from Turrenia the friends did not leave home again: they went straight to bed.

Then there were trips up the Mountain. These were more boisterous occasions, because they went skiing, ate al fresco, and looked down on Natàca far off on the plain as upon a very horrid trap from which they had at last managed to escape. The girls grew mettlesome, launched little screams into the air, and whirled about on the snow like a flock of cranes about to wing their flight to far-distant skies. Such days never passed without leaving some memory worth having.

Then there was dancing in the café at Brighella, a village half-way down the Mountain . . . No blows were spared in the effort to kill time; nor had these blows gone wide of the mark, if half the winter was already dead for ever.

Snow. Rodolfo's younger brother Enzo came home rubbing his hands and stamping his feet. "Freezing, out! . . . What are you up to? Working? I've been with Tommasini. The very devil, that chap. Now he's got his claws into old Cavaliere Areni, and managed to put it across him that the choirgirls have all fallen in love with him because they find him so noble and distinguished. Yesterday morning Via Messina, where the old boy lives, woke up to find itself baptized Via Cavaliere Areni . . . During the night Tommasini had stuck a bit of cardboard with the 'new' name over the old street-sign. When his sign was ripped down Tommasini wrote a protest to the papers, demanding that 'for the honour of the city' Via Messina should revert to being called Via Cavaliere Areni, and signing it 'A Resident of Via Cavaliere Areni' . . . What a crew they are! They've made poor old Testaccio believe he's a medium, and that the sublime spirits have cured his diabetes. The poor dumb cluck gobbles sugar by the handful, and maintains that the pains in his legs are simply the base spirits reluctant to climb out of his socks. But even from thence the sublime spirits will oust them! . . . What a crew, I tell you. One of the gang, Reitano in fact, came up to me with that nasal twang and shifty manner of his, and 'Listen you,' he hissed. 'I saw you in a dream last night. You were hanging on a cross, dressed up to the nines, stone dead.'"

Although Enzo was smiling he had turned unnaturally pale.

"You would be wise to have nothing to do with those louts," admonished Rodolfo. "You pretend it's fun, but you get home white as a sheet."

"Don't be an ass." Enzo frowned, and struck the pose he always did when he was stuck for an answer – bolt upright, feet together, slowly raising his head as though sniffing the air as high as was humanly possible. Generally speaking a spiritless, unassuming young man, he contrived a note of weary gaiety and declared that it pleased him to study those poor lunatics. He set about spouting names of writers who might conceivably do them justice, but the moment he mentioned one, he rejected it: all were too lightweight for a task as imposing as were those dear, queer characters with whom lock, stock and barrel he was willing to spend his livelong days.

"Sit down," snapped Rodolfo. "And don't go out in galoshes when it's not raining."

"No, it's not raining, but it's freezing cold . . . Yesterday Tommasini . . ."

Enzo took an armchair, remaining hat on head and hand on the crook of his umbrella. He then proceeded to give a long, detailed account of the trick Tommasini had played on some café-owner.

Rodolfo, muffled in a shawl, alternately lent an ear to his brother and traced lines on a sheet of paper.

For the Affluent Client had sent word that in the spring he would be in a position to entrust Rodolfo with some very important commissions . . . "I can hardly imagine anything will come of it," Rodolfo said to himself. "On the other hand, what would I do in Rome? At least there's a ghost of a client here in Natàca."

This ghost of a client, however, had to be transformed into a real live client. The game had some appeal: how to turn the ghost of a client into a real live one. Rodolfo made up his mind to spend a year in Natàca.

Was this then (Rodolfo gazed about him), was this then the precise instant when he was of his own accord deciding to stay another year in Natàca? How had it happened?

"Hmm!" thought Rodolfo. "Ask me another!"

Snow. Leonardo was alone and stranded among the spindly ash trees. His ski-boots encumbered him like a couple of dogs with legs braced against the pull of a leash. The mountain shone

– surpassing whiteness! – with a few clouds down below lazily drifting, or huddled nose to tail like sheep shepherded to the roadside for a cart to pass. And the silence of it all! Close at hand an azure sky, over there a silvery white, still further off all rosy and shimmering. The copse, ashtree and fir, greenery trailing from frail, worm-eaten wood, while the branches bore hundreds of nests of snow. The ashtree Leonardo had leant against gave a gentle creak, for the snow was melting, falling from topmost to lowest branch, all down the trunk to the gnarled roots . . . What had this kind of thing meant to him once upon a time? Leonardo tried to recall, to think back, to delve in his memory. What it had meant was childhood, the Christmas crib, his mother's pure face, the vague sound that told his heart to beat just this way or that way, as an instrument already tuned strikes up more rounded, more full, with more intensity than one still off pitch. Once upon a time . . . Ah, how it chops and changes, this perfidious life!

Some years are good, some bad. There are years when though nothing actually disagreeable happens everything seems dead and done for; and others when despite worries, and even disasters, a rosy promise prevails. Such ups and downs leave a man bewildered, inconsistent. The most important thing in life, according to Leonardo (who was at present trying to button up his glove with his teeth), the important thing in life boiled down to this: to be either a pessimist or an optimist. Why not be permanently one or the other? Why keep chopping and changing year in year out? Why be a travesty of oneself, forced to think with loathing today of yesterday's pronouncements, and mingle tomorrow with those whom we ridicule today.

Silence, what silence and solitude . . . But lo! at the rim of the valley there materializes a black speck. It grows, it draws nigh, it takes a shape, a Cossack figure, though rapidly softening and revealing itself to be that of a woman, tall, young and beautiful: the figure of Lisa Careni.

"Hullo there, Leo," she panted, performing a half-circle round his tree. "What on earth are you doing all alone here? No skis! Boots full of snow!"

"I'm just about to have lunch."

"Lunch?" The girl smiled. "*I* see no lunch. Still the same old fibber?"

"Still? Why *still*?"

Lisa laboured up to him, pushing on her ski-sticks. "Because you're not leaving after all. Why ever not? Fed up with work?"

Leonardo gave her a look. Lisa had blue eyes, but so deep and expressive as to appear almost black. A wisp of blond hair hung waiting to be tucked back under her fur cap. She was panting away freely.

Leonardo moved nearer, then, tilting his head on one side as if settling a fiddle under his chin and preparing to play a truly mournful melody, he began:

"Lisa dear, you're so kind and understanding. To you I can open my heart . . . The fact is, I cannot, at this moment, leave."

"Why on earth not? You're still out of sorts?"

"No, it seems I've recovered. At least, that's the result of my check-up."

"And you're not convinced?"

"Maybe I am . . . but . . . *you're* not laughing, you're not like the rest of them . . . You see, I'm still missing something absolutely basic."

Lisa removed her fur cap and knitted her winsome brow. "I don't follow you," she said.

"There's no joy in me!"

"Now I'm *really* lost. What joy isn't in you?"

"Oh, it's so hard to explain! I must try not to laugh while I tell you and you mustn't laugh while you're listening . . . You see, I've lost the inner light that brightens the path, that helps us see our way, that gives some meaning to what we're doing. It's not there. Look, I may seem to be talking gibberish, but when you've thought about something for too long your head fills up with fancy phrases . . . You see, I don't appear to have a sanction, an authoritative sanction, to live."

"Fancy stuff, fancy stuff!" exclaimed the girl. "Are you sure these aren't just obsessions?"

"That's not the point, Lisa. Naturally, if a fellow finds himself in a stagnant situation then whatever he thinks about is likely, even bound, to become an obsession."

"Fancy stuff, very fancy stuff," objected the girl, knitting her brow still further and struggling to shake one foot loose from its ski in order to stamp it impatiently. "No joy in you, eh? Well, nor has anyone else – at least, not as much as they'd like. So what? Do they bury themselves in the provinces, stop work, stop living?"

Leonardo again tilted his head until his ear brushed his shoulder.

"But I'm not talking about those bursts of high spirits, which are pretty rare in any case. I mean a continuous, day-by-day presence of joy, which allows for suffering, and hope, and despair, without seriously interrupting that perpetual state of bliss."

"Fancy stuff! Either you're on about something physical – in which case we see eye to eye, because naturally someone with a pain when there's nothing wrong with him is a different case from someone feeling the same pain who really is ill. Or you're talking about something else entirely, which I for one have never experienced."

"Maybe you have, but you're not aware of it because it's never left you."

"No, no, no, no!" cried the girl, with vigorous shakes of the head. "You've got obsessions. Don't tell me you're getting like so many of our precious fellow-townsmen, obsessed with your own finger, or crossing yourself, or keeping out the cold with newspapers."

"Lisa my dear, I'm in such a state I can't achieve anything useful or satisfying."

"You bet, Leo dear, seeing you do not a stroke of work and

spend your time strolling up and down the Corso morning, noon and night!"

"No, I *do* do some work from time to time, but it doesn't help. A man can be in such a state that although he gets up early, reads, writes, goes out, rushes around, shouts his head off, shuffles things about, he in fact gets nothing done and is a layabout. It takes a definite mood, a disposition that comes from within, a full consent of mind, for a man doing a few given things (and taking hours off into the bargain), really to be able to call himself a useful person, a worker and – in a word – a man at all."

"You're not going to tell me that what's needed is the dear old Joy?"

"Could be . . ."

"O Leo, you were such a quicksilver lad in the old days. Do you remember at the sea, when we used to sit on that upturned boat? One afternoon you'd begun to tell me you loved me but, would you believe it, someone bunged a fistful of sand into your mouth and by the time you'd finished spitting it out you'd lost your thread. So tell me now, now that we're older – when you said that, were you joking?"

Leonardo had drifted off into reveries of those times and, struck by a sense of religious awe at that oddly bold character who had a few years ago masqueraded under his name, he began to babble, "Those days . . . the boat . . . you . . . yes . . . no . . . No, I wasn't joking . . . I did love you . . . Still do . . . But things are different now. I'd be ashamed to spend even one whole day in your presence. Just now I'm so . . . ugly. I feel ugly to the marrow of my bones."

"But you *are* fond of me?"

"Yes."

"Do you mean it?" Lisa stuffed her hands away to hide the trembling. Then, calmer, she put on her cap and sped off downhill, leaving a sparkling whirligig in the air.

Leonardo's eyes followed her for a long time. Such eyes! Too dulled and weak, like tattered spiders' webs, to hold so much as a gnat for long. But in the old days, ah then! then he knew that his eyes shot forth something living, unswerving, penetrating, glad. He felt then, when he looked at a thing, that it was made radiant by his look, and was in bliss, as he was.

Snow. Giovanni Luisi took the advice of Professor Meloni, according to whom one could make whole hours pass by smoking a pipeful of cigarette tobacco and poking the embers in the brazier with the tongs: "You concentrate, the mind begins to flow . . ." The flames in an open fire, leaping hither and thither, flaring up, dying down, are in the long run distracting, but those glowing coals, like staring eyes among the cinders, bestow a wondrous patience. You can spend hours and hours this way. And seeing that when you get up from your chair you are still under the influence of those coals, that calm, that patience, that tranquillity, it can be said that this is the way to spend the rest of the winter, and shake yourself out of it only in early April.

And indeed, here is April. The albums of the damsels of Natàca, which piously preserve the maxims and signatures of total strangers – since these damsels imagine that anyone coming from the North to lecture in Natàca must be an Immortal and, blushing, trembling and stuttering, have begged for his autograph – the albums of these young ladies bear inscriptions such as, "I met you one radiant moment, and you are lovely as an April day!"

April in Natàca was queer and unpredictable, one moment overcast and the next a shining mirror. Towards the end of the month, in a single burst, came the warm weather. The snow melted off the Mountain in a day, and with it the excursions, the ski-races, the descents *à deux*, the rare happy moments, a reason for living.

At the beginning of May the sky grew heavy, the air close, and the odour of the citrus blossom no longer had a chink to escape through: the sea cast it back at Natàca, the Mountain drove it back on Natàca, the upper air clamped down on it. This odour, thus compressed, pressed in turn upon the nerves of the Natàcans. Now it was that the girls became all overwrought, took to fanning themselves with their fingers, and as they passed along the street looked not in the shop windows but at the boys, raking them with their eyes from stem to stern. The damsels now were seized by strange perturbations which caused them constantly to hear their own names called aloud. They ran to the door, they ran to the telephone, they ran to the window. But no one had called to them, and back they would come all rapt in thought. Many put on so much weight in a couple of weeks that you'd have thought some wag was inflating them by sheer lung-power, others wasted away with the speed of a burning candle; some who were beautiful woke up ugly, whilst others, who were ugly, stepped into their shoes. All things physical were in unspeakable unrest and confusion. The faces of Erasmo Veni and Enzo De Mei erupted into masses of tiny little white faces, apparently about to give birth to dozens of other Erasmos and Enzos.

It was beyond all human power to stay indoors during waking hours: the streets permitted only momentary homecomings. Stretched out on the iron benches the young men dreamt out loud. The voices of the street rose up, and the denizens of the first-floors-up had minute knowledge of all the nightbirds' thoughts about Miss Elsa or Miss Nina, the dreams they'd had about them, the dreams they hoped to have, and how it would be if those dreams came true on a pleasure cruise. O ships, O trains, O aeroplanes . . . At the vaudeville, when someone came up for the third time with "Let's be off to Barcelona!" the audience was swept by a subdued roar, like a concourse of lions to which a passing child has unthinkingly pointed out the presence of a suckling calf.

"Barcelona?" was the cry. "Barcelona? We'd go to hell itself if hell were at least three days away."

Said Signora Luisi to her son Giovanni: "My son, you have your own way to make in this world, don't give a thought to *us*. If you must leave you must, and God go with you. No, no! Have no thought for us, we are old, and have already had our day. I, for my own part, feel I have no further use here below. When you have left, the Lord will do me a favour by taking me to Him. Because, you see, I am old, your father is old . . . After seven in the evening we expect no more callers, we bar the door. When you are around your father says to me, 'Don't bar the door dear, because the lad's still out.' He knows I know that perfectly well, but he also knows that I like to be reminded of it. We get into bed, but we keep an ear cocked for the key, waiting for you to come in with those tiptoeing footsteps that haven't changed since you were ten years old, and you go to the bathroom and brush your teeth, and then the sound of your bedroom door opening and shutting. We even hear the click of your light when you switch it off a whole hour later (why *do* you read so much at night?), and then we say 'The dear boy's gone to sleep!' and I think of the coffee-pot ready and waiting on the stove, and tomorrow I have only to light the gas and wait two minutes before I bring you up your cup . . . But when you're not here the day's over and done with at seven, we go off to bed and your father, poor thing, never says another word. We don't get to sleep, of course, our thoughts are on you, we are thinking that you're grown-up now and have no more use for those two old fogies all wasting away and shrivelled with the cold, feeling so tiny in that great bed of theirs . . . What use *are* we then? Yes, you must leave, go off and have fun, and never think (no, not for a moment!) of what we are doing or what has become of us. But may the Lord soon gather me to His bosom! . . . So, cheer up!"

"Cheer up?" gulped Giovanni, eyes awash with tears. "Cheer

up, eh? Thanks a lot! You've bequeathed me a lifetime of happiness with this harangue of yours. Please go on. Please don't consider my feelings! . . ."

He left his chair, tottered slowly down the corridor, entered his room, gazed in the mirror. Why should this man with grizzling hair force so many memories upon the best-loved Darby and Joan on the face of the planet? Why should it be that without that face (of which incidentally the mirror reflected an ashen image), that without that face he would willingly have swapped for another, without that inane face beside them, those two old folks would feel at death's door?

He left his room and returned to the study. His mother smiled up at him.

"I'm not going away," announced Giovanni.

"Besides," he added to himself, "whenever the general does deign to see me he has nothing to tell me, but begs that I remain assured that he is the most luckless of men – having made so many promises over the last months, he still has no decent paid job to offer me – and implores me to condole with him . . . Well, he can jolly well beg for sympathy elsewhere!"

VIII

TOWARDS THE END OF MAY began the heat, a fierce, afflicting heat that never lets up until the end of September. Like seafood being boiled alive men grew ever more sluggish in their movements while their eyes, covered with a fine but perpetual film, harboured a weariness and a wish to see nothing. Others, taking their walk towards six in the evening, reminded one less of fish than of woodcock dangling dead from a hunter's hand.

Every so often came a swift fiery wind out of Africa, the dreaded "south wind". The piazzas were so scorching that leaving home in the morning the barefoot children seared the soles of their feet, and yelped as if skipping on the bricks of an oven. In a brace of shakes they had made newspaper bundles of their feet, and were walking with slow, gingerly tread, trailed by the most savage curs in the area, which were wearied by the weather, tamed, in need of a master. The citizens of Natàca sought relief at the seaside, whither they were borne by a procession of trams, as slowly and jouncingly as crates on carts carrying fowls from village to village. The air thinned out and in the apt phraseology of Masolino Ricasoli (a young comic writer, Natàca-born but resident in Milan and well-known throughout Italy), "people's brains bubble in their skulls like fizzy water in neck of a bottle when the cork pops" . . . The sea grew dull and brackish, and such was the humidity that you constantly felt you were fingering the belly of a bat.

★

"Paulus!" exclaimed Professor Neri, stopping Paolo Filesi in his tracks, "hearken unto this: Paulus – Peter and Paul – Peter's Pence – i.e. 'donation'. Slip me a lira and we'll say no more about it."

Filesi fished out the lira, with a smile at Leonardo, who didn't have the heart to smile back.

Professor Neri was the seventh man of genius they had met in the course of the morning. The brainy set were all a-seething. Men of art and science were in a state of grace which instilled awe and respect. Take, for instance, Avvocato De Marchi. He was crying aloud for a music-master to transcribe a symphony he had created in a single night and now held in all its entirety in his head. "It's all in here, in here!" he cried, tapping his forehead with two fingers, anxious lest at any moment his brow should emit a hollow boom, sure signal that the symphony had evaporated. "It's here, the whole thing, from the first note to the last. For heaven's sake find me a maestro to get it down on paper before it escapes me, vanishes! Isn't there a single music-master in this god-forsaken town?"

"Of course there is. Calm down, your honour," said Tommasini. "Leave it all to me." And that same evening he called on De Marchi in the company of a sea-captain who claimed to be a piano virtuoso and graduate of the Prague Conservatoire and then proceeded to fill a foolscap notebook with squiggles.

Old Leopoldi had at long last invented perpetual motion. It went like this: if you fill a bottle with water almost up to the cork but not quite, what happens? A gap forms in the neck. If you upturn the bottle the water fills the neck but the gap appears at the bottom. If you then stand the bottle upright the gap moves into the neck again. Now imagine filling the same bottle with gas, up to the cork but not quite. Gasses, as everyone knows, tend instantly to fill any gap in the receptacle containing them. What, therefore, will occur? If the gap is in the neck of the bottle the gas will rush to fill it, but a similar gap will appear at the bottom; the gas will rush towards the bottom, and the gap will reappear at the top. Again the gas will rush, but the gap will always reappear, so that the gas will be ever on the move. *Voilà!* Perpetual motion . . .

Leopoldi was trying to scrounge the money to go to Rome to expound his discovery, in the minutest detail, to His Majesty the King.

Meanwhile, Nereggia had written a sacred drama on the theme of Santa Genoveffa, patron saint of the city, and was waiting for the Archbishop to reply to his humble request for a private audience: "Stating the day and the hour, mind you! The day and the hour!" The voluminous manuscript containing twenty-one thousand lines of blank verse, every blessed one of them ending with a proparoxytonic, was in the meantime being bound in vellum.

There was also the wealthy Cavaliere De Filippi, author of the volume *Funny Jokes*, notorious for having (in vain) offered a small fortune to a leading Milan newspaper to publish on the "Culture Page" a photograph of himself bearing the caption "De Filippi, the great dialect poet". This wealthy gentleman had gone on a tour of the hill-villages in his automobile, shepherding around Francesco De Sanctis, Anatole France, Ferdinando Martini and . . . Nello Tommasini. Now and again he enquired, "Do you really think an article from you, a single article, would be sufficient to put my reputation on a pretty firm footing?" And the bewhiskered person who, according to Tommasini's introduction, answered to the name of Francesco De Sanctis, mumbled, "Oh, by Jove yes, more than enough!"

The Corso milled with people anxious for enlightenment as to whether *Aïda* was not more beautiful than *Parsifal*; whether records played backwards from the last note to the first might not give birth to prodigious new symphonies; whether it was really and truly true that Manzoni's *I Promessi Sposi* wasn't all it was cracked up to be. Or perhaps, as to whether it was true that the Great Lizard had a real Parisian mistress; that the Republic of San Marino had requested as its president a citizen of Natàca, to wit a certain Sugarloaf Maled, known to some as "the king" because he claimed a right to the throne of

England, and to others as "the horse" because of his prancing gait and habit of snorting; whether it was true there were cemeteries on the new ocean liners . . . And so on and so forth.

Rosso Autini, away on a Mediterranean cruise, where naturally enough he had not attained his whole object in setting foot on board, which was to avoid the hell of the heat, sent his friends letters and telegrams from every port. From Istanbul he wrote: "D'you know why Marconi committed suicide? . . . Because he invented the wireless, but couldn't manage to invent a stringless yo-yo." The contents of this letter had been broadcast far and wide in Natàca, and now at every corner in the Corso somebody was asking somebody else, "D'you know why Marconi committed suicide?"

Leonardo, dog-tired, began talking gibberish – asking if it wouldn't be only proper to take a sub-machine-gun and pepper those loafers against the walls and in the shop doorways. Finally he said goodbye to Paolo Filesi, went home, threw himself on a bed dank with sirocco and drew the sheet over his head. But he failed to exclude the voices from the street, one of which came to him still clarion clear: "D'you know why Marconi committed suicide?"

Lisa Careni, in her back garden at home, beneath the sardonic gaze of the dog Dora, was practising archery. She was a dead shot, pinning lizards to the wall and leaving them desperately jerking their heads back and forth. Then she hurled away the bow and stamped to the house to drum on a window-pane. Oh, the boredom and horror of it all!

Her sister Maria picked up the bow, drew it, and let fly. But the arrow went wide and flew over the wall. Shortly afterwards there it was again, in the hand of a dark-eyed youngster who, bowing politely, presented it to Maria.

"Forgive me," murmured the young man, "if I take the liberty of returning this . . ."

"Are you apologizing for doing a favour?"

Maria looked him over and, as if a ray of light had revealed her future, with perfect serenity said to herself: "I'm going to marry this man."

"Thanks," she said out loud. "Thank you very much."

The youngster went his way well contented. Lisa had not so much as turned her head. When her sister came up she was still drum-drumming on the window-pane.

"The boredom and horror of it all!" she hissed between clenched teeth.

Maria settled her mind on marriage as on a ship that might carry her far far away from that sea of boredom and horror.

"Oh, if only it were autumn!" moaned Lisa, bunching her fist and pounding *that* against the window.

As mothers warn their children not to stare overlong at the sky, since the heavens do not grant long life to those who fix their gaze on them, so our advice to the Natàcans would be to steer clear of phrases such as "When, O when will autumn come?" (Or spring, or what you will.) Because the seasons in Natàca don't have to be asked twice – two shakes of a lamb's tail and they're upon you.

Only yesterday did Lisa Careni say, "Oh, if only it were autumn!" and lo, autumn it is. In the park the leaves hang on the boughs like the leaves of other trees sewn on to them by silken threads. The sirocco creates a sky so ponderous that it seems a great spiders'-web is spun upon the rooftops, ready to press down ever further and trap those pathetic flies who are the Natàcans.

"September again," thought Leonardo. "It's last autumn I came back to Natàca, thinking to stay three weeks, and it's been a whole year! . . . Another September now, another autumn!"

Melancholy enough, these thoughts of having been in Natàca since last autumn, but swiftly to be outdated by the fact that it was no longer autumn but winter. The three towering plane-trees in the Corso gradually shed their leaves, but gradually, as they did so, acquired a graver and more noble aspect. As a venerable gentleman, his arms full of baubles picked up from children at play around his knees, when confronted by something really serious – a funeral, a beautiful woman, a High Court judge – drops the lot and stands there rigid, expressionless, ready to make the deepest of bows, so at the coming of the first black clouds stood each tall plane-tree in the Corso.

December. Hordes of barefoot children would soon come swarming in from the outlying villages with basketfuls of tiny models of the Infant Jesus, and the bagpipes would send their baa-lamb baas right up the stairwells to the skylights thick with stars. The sirocco was rinsed away by the winds of the new year. Everyone could watch his own personal star winking at him from on high. What did Leonardo's tell him? What promise did theirs hold for Rodolfo or Giovanni or Paolo Filesi? Each had chosen the biggest and brightest in the firmament of Natàca, so no wonder if, unwittingly, all four of them now had the selfsame star.

IX

ONCE YOU HAVE LEARNT to get through a year, you become more skilled in the art of killing time. Admittedly, you have no fun; admittedly, you are bored to tears. But there is a weird bitter fun that defeats all description to be had from that uniform non-enjoyment and monotony. The soul contracts alliances the more stubborn for being secret and unmentionable. All things conspired towards staying on in Natàca – even all that chat about travelling (for which they gradually developed a fondness), and all that yearning to escape from Natàca which, if they really got away, would create a void nothing else could fill. Furthermore, once they had acquired such skill at killing time it was no easy matter to give it up (for it was the most perfect expression of their personal moral qualities and cast of mind), and go off to some place where that skill would be bound to perish since time passes there of its own accord.

Our quartet of friends had perfected the art of sleep. Which of us has not wished to be able at will to bury his head in sleep and play the ostrich whenever his waking eye falls on something disagreeable? Very well, our friends now knew a particular way of closing their eyes and carrying out a few mental manoeuvres which brought on sleep in a trice, like darkness when you puff out an oil-lamp. They also felt, in their sleep, when it wished to leave them, and knew how to hang onto it with their teeth like a blanket which someone else is tugging at the foot of.

They also practised another exercise. They would say to themselves for example, "Last year, I was really quite upset by all those carnival dances with nothing but chaps in trousers and other chaps dressed up in petticoats. This year I bet they won't make me turn a hair!" And by exerting considerable will-power, they succeeded in their intent.

Then again: "Those cafés crowded with stuffed dummies; those intimate secrets shouted around the streets; Rosso Autini's harangues and Tommasini's pranks; the black mack, the black galoshes, the black umbrella, the black gloves in which, even on sunny days, Enzo De Mei stirs abroad; that business of walking hundreds of times past the same cracked mirror in the Corso and a hundred times seeing your own face split in half, the two halves out of kilter; and the autumn sirocco . . . last year these things really upset me, whereas this year I'm going to make them feel perfectly normal."

And they succeeded.

To all this they added Christian charity. What right had they to think ill of people who always sat around or slouched about with their hands in their pockets, laughing fit to bust or playing horrid jokes on each other? Were not even they God's creatures? Would it not be a real challenge to learn to love them?

A real challenge! Words irresistible to noble spirits! Who ever has refused himself to an experiment, even of the pottiest, if it was presented to him as "a real challenge"?

Thus, little by little, they contrived to find charm and amiability even in Nello Tommasini, Enzo De Mei, Rosso Autini, Nereggia, Professor Neri, Avvocato De Marchi, Leopoldi, and even that Wire-Whiskered Willie who, left alone one night in his chop-house with the last customer, a half-drunk, half-asleep dotard, brandished a kitchen knife and forced the man to swallow one by one no fewer than twenty-nine prickly pears.

Needless to say, what lent the most piquant savour to this Christian sentiment was not pity. Pity might have given offence. Out upon it! And little by little something akin to admiration crept into its place. They began to say that no other town could produce characters as vivid, varied and full of "human interest" as Wire-Whiskered Willie, Leopoldi or Tommasini. Leonardo went so far as to formulate this *pensée*: "Having friends in other towns, after friends in Natàca, is like drinking a glass of watered wine after one at 24 degrees of alcohol."

And so our friends' second year in Natàca had nothing new to offer and was no more and no less than the first, with slightly fewer unpleasant reactions to the same, perfectly identical events. The only thing worth mentioning is that on Christmas Eve Leonardo and Rodolfo had a mind to play a noteworthy trick on themselves. They bought a *panettone*, one of those rich, spongy Christmas cakes as big as a football, retired to a small room, sat down face to face with knife in hand, and by sheer will-power (will-power, as we see, was much employed in Natàca), slowly slowly slice by slice they cut and devoured the whole enormous confection, until their eyes were popping out of their heads.

The third year in Natàca was identical to the second, and since the psyche, at the mere remembrance of the crisp commands it had received the previous year, agreed to smile at this episode or that, the year became almost an enjoyable one.

The winter was cold but clear. Trips up the Mountain came thick and fast. Leonardo, Rodolfo, Giovanni and Paolo were by this time veteran skiers: they clambered up, they shot down, they made fast runs, they launched themselves from considerable heights, they fell clumsily but not badly enough to cause severe injury. In the evenings, dancing at the Careni's. Maria had become engaged to the dark-eyed young man who had retrieved that errant arrow. Dora the dog had lain down and died on the feet of Professor Luigini – a dear old bald buffer (poet, author, and teacher of Greek), tranquil of heart and steady of mind; which prompted Leonardo to comment that "What Dora was really looking for was a *happy* man on whose feet she could lay her soul."

Meantime the days sped by, and they sped smoothly. Our

friends were all smiles, as if they had been toiling to turn a great wheel, and now saw it revolving all on its own without a sound, or rather with the hum of bees which is so pleasant and persuasive . . .

One afternoon, however, Rodolfo arrived breathless at Giovanni's. He had something to tell, something urgent, as if it were a piece of news he had just received that gave him the creeps.

"Calm down," said Giovanni, switching off the wireless and stretching. "What's up?"

"Life!"

"Life, eh?"

"Yes, life! It's slipping away . . ."

"What d'you mean, slipping away? *What* life?"

"Ours. It's slipping away. We talk about killing time, but we're really only killing ourselves."

"Has that only just dawned on you?"

"Come on, don't laugh! It's not a matter of anything *dawning*. I feel it in my bones, I see it before my very eyes as plain as a pikestaff: life's slipping away. It's criminal! Youth and life, we only get them the once, and they're slipping away . . ."

"You propose to stop them?"

"Not stop them, but not chuck them away either, and for no reason at all."

"Oh, for goodness sake think about something else."

But Giovanni too was troubled, as when a small child chants "Someone's left the tap on! The house is under water!" and at first you smile, then you hear the noise of water and things splashing and bashing about – and then you run!

They were both on their feet now, Giovanni pacing round the table, Rodolfo watching him with scared eyes. They crossed to the window and noisily threw the shutters open. The sun was setting, and the last red ray stretched right across the room, but swiftly vanished, as does a headlight beam from a passing car.

Rodolfo shuddered. "Let's close 'em," he said.

★

So, whether it slips away or sprints or ambles, according to our literary wit Masolino Ricasoli, down from Milan for a day or two, life is "a liquid which very often goes murky on you," but which he personally had no trouble at all in clarifying. Masolino possessed infallible remedies: you chase away "night thoughts" with a hot bath, a bad taste in the morning with a spoonful of fruit salts. If your brain is overworked, two Recresal tablets; if suffering from melancholy, twenty drops of Forgenine. You are losing weight? A course of Promonta. So well did he know the doses his own body needed at any one moment that he went so far as to mess up his own metabolism for fun and then, in a brace of shakes, make it all as right as rain again.

Masolino had such a sprightly, witty way of talking, such a way of throwing figures of speech together, the goodly with the ghastly, truth with trumpery, that Leonardo positively enjoyed going for walks with him along the abandoned tramlines of Via Cavour. When in Milan Masolino followed a strict diet, but in Natàca even he was obliged to stuff himself with the vast repasts of the South; at which more often than not, especially on festive occasions, roast kid was served. Indeed, unfailingly so.

"The kid, that mildest of creatures," observed Masolino, "is in reality a ferocious beast which leaves its victims no peace for at least three days. Now at this moment, you see me walking, talking and smoking; yet here," and he gestured towards his stomach, "lies the kid, good as gold, head between hooves."

A couple of hours later, halted in his tracks by a sudden fit of vertigo, "It's the kid," he groaned, leaning on Leonardo. "It's come to life. It's jumping around inside me." And late that evening, as he sipped at a lemonade: "Ouch! Argh! The kid knows the game is up, it abhors lemon juice, it's maddened with rage, it's trampling me to bits!"

The following day, with a sigh of relief, he announced that his struggle with the kid was taking a turn for the better. Leonardo also tried to play the buffoon in a similar fashion, but never quite brought it off . . .

Masolino (amongst other observations of interest) one evening came out with this: that "he who cometh to Natàca rarely departeth." The air was unctuous and cloying, making one feel as though wading through honey. He, for example, ought by rights to have left town the previous evening, but hadn't quite managed to snap shut the catches of his cases – how could he put it? – he had no strength in his thumb. Attempts to close his baggage, repeated today, had produced results which, though an improvement, had not been conclusive. Masolino had hopes of succeeding in his enterprise the day after tomorrow.

"You're dead right," agreed Leonardo. "I came down here for three weeks, and I've stayed three years."

"Take it from me, you're tied by one foot to the Town Hall of Natàca. You're like a captive golf-ball that may be whacked as far as Milan even, but at full stretch, at a single bound it'll whiz back here."

"Dead right!" said Leonardo with a laugh.

One afternoon, still chuckling at Masolino, he set off for Rome. On reaching his hotel he was seized by a hollow feeling, a dizzy sickness. Not a morsel could he force between his lips, let alone swallow. "Just you wait and see," he laughed to himself. "No sleep for you tonight!" And still in the grip of that laugh, which rang hollower and hollower, he spent a white night, his heart thumping in his breast, nausea, the room dancing in circles and Masolino's dictum buzzing round and round in his head.

The third day he fled Rome and returned to Natàca. During the journey it began to rain. Eyes fixed on the rain-streaked windows, the drops descending silently, little by little he calmed down. His nausea gradually waned and gave place to appetite. Things that had been shimmery before now became solid and reliable: "It's going to take a year or two more in Natàca." He ought never to have left before the light returned, the *joie de vivre*. There was a touch of mystery in the whole business.

In that very same period Paolo Filesi, with a triumphant grin, announced that his luggage was already in Rome, in the flat he had rented for the year, and that he would be hard on its heels. He was the envy of his friends, who saw him home every night as a mark of respect and homage towards one who was off to reside in the capital, and as a token of affection for a departing friend. The young lawyer preserved a modest and benevolent demeanour; he maintained that Natàca was by no means to be despised; that even in Natàca it was possible to have adventures – speaking for himself, he had had many.

"Gosh, when?" wondered his friends, who knew the whole course of his life hour by hour and minute by minute.

On the morning he was due to leave, an intravenous injection – the last of a course Paolo had been taking to discourage his girl-friends in Rome (imitating the singsong accent of Natàca) from asking "Paolo, why are you such a stringbean?" – this pointless injection in the groin went bad on him. Result, blood-poisoning and fever. Gradually the poor young man's face glazed over with an expression so profoundly calm and ethereal, a smile so endearing, though at the same time so remote and mysterious, that his friends exchanged silent glances. What was afoot? After a while a few whispers began to meander about the room and Paolo, from the depths of his bed, appeared to be watching them – impossible to imagine that he could himself be uttering them, since his lips were all but motionless, and only his eyes roved slowly about the ceiling.

On the third day Paolo became delirious. He begged his father to open a drawer in the next room – at the far end on the right – and to burn the duchess's letters. What duchess? What letters? Both were pure fantasy. This indeed was death, a meaningless death from a meaningless injection. How could this poor young man have come to such an end? Something there is in the universe that likes its little joke, and has the power to kill us.

Leonardo, Rodolfo and Giovanni were prostrated. Paolo was no more. A genuine bitterness that the only reminders of such a kind, gentle, engaging young fellow were the high silk collars on show in the shop-windows, the "excuse me's", the cups of tea. In the midst of grief they simply had to smile, because this catastrophe in a way smacked of a dirty trick. Smiling, however, lent poignancy to grief, and the dirty trickery worsened the catastrophe.

A month dragged by, wretchedly. Then came an unexpected lull. Some evenings, in the Luisi's dining-room, while the wireless was pouring forth soft waltzes from Vienna, it seemed to them that things were growing so clear . . . so clear that from one moment to the next the mighty secret of the universe would stand revealed.

Except that one Sunday, late at night, when the gangs of youths who'd found nothing amusing to do met up in the semi-deserted Corso, each seeing the others as they saw themselves, stray dogs scrabbling in the dirt in case the bone they hadn't found under the table might be there in the streets; while these gangs were calling lugubriously to one another, "Haven't you got homes? . . . Go to bed then!", Giovanni was seized by such frenzy, such impatience, such distress, that he couldn't hold it in.

"We're never going to leave!" he burst out. "There's no escape from Natàca! We're here to stay. We'll die here. This town's a trap. It'll never let us go!"

"Take it easy," said Rodolfo. "Don't talk bilge. I mean one *can* live even here . . ."

"You can live here as long as you know you're free to live somewhere else. If not, this place is a prison."

They turned into a sidestreet – Giovanni really seemed to have gone off his rocker.

"Our mothers," he yelled, "our blasted mothers get younger every day, while we grow old before our time. They only think of themselves. Their sole concern is keeping us tied to their apron-strings. Hearing us come home at night – that's their only purpose in life. But the purpose of *our* lives can't possibly be letting our mothers hear our padding feet!"

"Idiot!" said Rodolfo. "Your own mother was the first to advise you to get out."

"Ho ho, she advised me all right, but then, I don't know why not, none of us manages to escape. That's the truth of the matter. We're trapped."

"Why," asked Leonardo gently, "should you say 'trap' of a large city with seaside and mountain and several hundred thousand inhabitants? Why should life here be all that awful? Lots of people would love to spend their days and their evenings as we do."

"Our evenings! In the dining-room! With that smell of prunes? I can't get the whiff of it off me! When I die, I'm convinced death will be something that starts with the smell of prunes. To hell with the lot of 'em!"

"But listen," objected Leonardo. "One of these days we'll be off. But in our own time, when we really have to. The important thing is to find a spot of work here in Natàca. Not that we're completely shiftless. We've all got something to do in our way – me with my bits for the papers, Rodolfo with his drawings, you keeping an eye on the family firm. But we have to find something with more dignity to it, some aim for all our united efforts; something that takes love and sacrifice, and not just slogging along. Then we'll have a real job, and be happy in it. We'll be working as a group. And something tells me that this job is soon going to turn up."

Leonardo's instincts served him well, for in the near future a very important person was to arrive in Natàca, a person destined to leave his mark, not only in the memories of the townsfolk, but also on the skyline of the city: a personage destined to provide a single purpose to a thousand different people and, incidentally, to our story.

Anyway, Giovanni soon simmered down. He sat on some church steps and started to think the exact opposite of what he had thought five minutes earlier. He cheerfully returned to his pet notion: that one of these days the general would find him a position worthy of him, and until he had procured it he himself could look upon the world with the superiority of a master not yet recognized by his dog. The exceptional person he took himself to be, in his youth his boon companion, from whom he had been parted with much regret, suddenly reappeared to keep him company.

"What a fool I've been being!" he laughed, and claimed that the whole of that weepy speech had only been a joke at his friends' expense.

Leonardo and Rodolfo laughed along with him. For a whole hour they went around elbowing each other and yelling each other's names, pretending that they might be heard by their parents, asleep far off in their shuttered-up homes.

Then, in a better mood than usual, they wended their way home. A better mood because their hearts had promised them they would make no more childish scenes, would no longer be scared or angry or impatient, but would prepare to grow up in Natàca, placidly, as in any other place on earth.

PART TWO

I

THE TRAIN, after leaving the tunnel but before arriving at the station, speeds across a long, curving viaduct which commands a panoramic view of Natàca. The passengers get to their feet and go to the windows to admire on the one side Natàca and on the other the sea. There happened to be, on one occasion, two passengers on that train, the first of whom, Francesco Buscaino by name, got up and went to the window, whereas the second, whose name we are content to be innocent of, remained seated.

The passenger who stood up was a man of middle age, with a lean face and features so finely chiselled as to suggest that his creator, in conceiving and achieving it, had set himself to raise the standards of the human face and had spared himself neither time nor pains to reach his goal. Above this lean face the hair grew delicately, and even the moustaches – long and flowing – seemed attached to the lip by the sheer delight of being where they were.

His figure was neither tall nor broad, but evidenced the same careful fashioning as did the face. His body was almost entirely swathed in a green overcoat, pleasantly full above the belt, and below, draped and undulatory; while the hem was so low as barely to reveal the glitter of the shoes. On high, within an ample raised collar like the leaves around a magnolia flower, it supported the head of which we have spoken.

His luggage, by means of appropriate labels, indicated that in America not only had he stayed in the most de luxe hotels and edited a newspaper, but had enjoyed the friendship of a celebrated bishop who was in the habit of ordering his servant to adorn the luggage of favoured guests with a sticky label bearing the words "Blest be your travels and your sojourns!" . . . That not only had he undergone a sensational but far from dishonourable lawsuit, as a result of which he had returned for a visit to Italy, of which the labels strove to describe the astonishing vicissitudes, the glittering visits, the sensational holidays, but also that he was now fed up with living in Italy and was returning to America, where a great Hollywood movie company was clamouring for him to become its managing director. As we see, our traveller had so schooled his suitcases that it would have been out of place for him to speak harshly of the times when a gentleman seeking adventures in the world used to travel around with a chatterbox of a servant who, while pretending to run his master down, in fact rendered him interesting alike to hosts and to hostesses.

Buscaino, standing at the window, cast a look of misgiving over the city of Natàca. "What a town!" he thought. "All the houses like little flat boxes . . . Nothing upstanding . . . Oh, bless the skyscrapers! They may be as arrogant and spiky and hideous as you please, but they speak of a city on its feet, a city wide awake, a city ready and willing to march towards infinity!" (Readers should not be surprised at this eloquence, because one of our traveller's characteristics was to think and talk with more *élan*, and therefore better, than the rest of us.) "Low houses, low buildings. A town stretched out on the ground – worse still, a town asleep on the ground! The kind of people who need a helping hand up from the sand . . . Oh, how well do I know them. Many's the time I've swum in such a sea! . . . People capable of yawning even on their wedding night . . . People . . . And yet, simple, good-natured folk . . . Yes, naïve. I'm pretty sure that here, as in America, a man has a right to stop a stranger in the street with 'Say, I have an idea!' My God, in America your stranger leads you right into the nearest bar and says, 'What'll you have, Mr Buscaino? What's your choice? And now let's hear about this idea of yours.' Here, instead, they look at you with the eyes of a terminal patient, they smile sadly, but when it comes down to it even here they're impressed. Even here an idea is an idea . . . A city on its back, a town of little boxes . . . A skyscraper here? No, perhaps not a skyscraper . . . A tower . . . By God, now *that's* an idea!"

Our traveller was perfectly accustomed to having ideas, so he did not jump for joy; none the less his eye gleamed like an aperture beyond which something enormous has just taken an enormous leap.

"There's more gold in this idea than in all the mines of Westphalia: a tower, with an inside staircase . . . no, an outside staircase . . . but perhaps inside is better. But what does it matter, inside or out, as long as lots and lots of people can climb it and gaze out over the panorama of the city? Panorama of the city, panorama of the city! There's nothing people here won't do for a panorama of the city. Most of the postcards folks send home are of the panorama of the city . . . And what, after all, do painters paint? The panorama of the city! And when, on Holy Saturday, women throw their babies up into the air to make them grow and grow, what's the big idea? To make their babies grow so tall that they can see the panorama of the city . . . Very well, you shall view the panorama of your city from a tower one hundred and fifty feet high! You shall see the windows of your own homes, the roofs of the rooms you were born in, the smoke from the chimney where your own dinner is cooking! You will get some notion of the ridiculous great den you live in . . . And the churchbells which wake you all too early in the morning, you will see where the sound comes from and how far it travels; you will know the reason why your studies are hampered by that fairground music, why your drinking water is murky, why your dwelling is either damp or else a furnace, what cypress of ill-omen overshadows your home from afar, and therefore why your family has been afflicted by so many calamities. Open your eyes! You will in future have something to do on Sundays:

you'll be yawning less and stretching your legs more. There are three hundred thousand of you – three hundred thousand perfect sheep. You'll all pay two lire a head to climb up the tower (and I take no account of anyone who wants to climb up twice, or of tourists) . . . We shall have spent about one hundred thousand lire to put up the building, and into our coffers you will pour six hundred thousand. Thank you, thank you, thank you very much! The profit is positively vast . . . Enough to give pause not only to a man on his way to America, but to scores of souls on their way to heaven . . ."

Our traveller restlessly fingered the window-pane. Every nerve in body and mind had decided to alight at the station at Natàca. Even his suitcases had begun to wobble menacingly as if eager to tumble down . . . Our traveller, once stirred by a great idea, could no longer call himself a man, but rather a team of living beings fighting under the one name: that of Francesco Buscaino. See! his hands go to work, the right hand to prop up a note-pad against the window and scribble, "Must stop in Natàca for a couple of months, set up committee then Limited Company. By spring, tower should be built, so in June, back to America. Hurrah for life!" Meanwhile the left hand fishes out a pocket-watch from his waistcoat. His eyes for a moment scan the note-book, are then lowered to observe that it is ten in the morning, his lips murmur "Right then!", his feet swivel towards his luggage, his biceps bulge in readiness to haul it down, his chest swells with mighty breaths, his heart beats like the blows of a blacksmith in a hurry to straighten the horseshoe on his anvil. His mind advises him to put up at the best hotel in Natàca, to give a luncheon for the most prominent up-and-coming young fellows in town, to address them respectfully on every occasion, to give a lecture and, if possible, promote a picture exhibition.

In short, our traveller had become a whole regiment bursting with energy and eagerness which, at the first shudder of the train as it drew to a halt, leapt down onto the platform and shouted "Porter!"

II

THE HALL-PORTER at the Hotel Colonna was aware that Professor Buscaino would be staying in Natàca for two months, and would then be returning to America. He knew also that he was installed in a suite on the second floor, about which he had had many complaints to make; that he fed on unusual specialities, so that special crockery and glassware had to be bought for him. He knew, moreover, that for the first week he had been always alone, but that on the Monday of the second week he went up in the lift first with one friend, then with two, then three, then four . . . until finally there were so many friends that the lift stuck halfway up and the whole hotel heard Professor Buscaino's voice: "But these aren't hotels! This is no elevator! This is no sort of town at all! No one's moving a finger, no one bestirring themselves! I tell you gentlemen, that even in America similar misfortunes occur, but they are put right in a brace of shakes . . . Let us synchronize our watches, gentlemen, and you will tell me how many hours we shall have spent here . . . I remember that in Boston once, at the Great Central Hotel, an elevator got stuck between floors. I tell you all hell broke loose, and we had the satisfaction of hearing a pandemonium of firebells and sirens . . ."

The professor's friends were thereafter taken aloft in three instalments. What they were at, shut up in that second-floor suite for two or three hours at a time, no one was able to figure out.

On this particular day, however, they were all assembled in

the hotel lounge, round a table dotted with ashtrays and dishes of biscuits. The lounge doors, by express orders of Professor Buscaino, were shut fast.

Seated round the tables were Leopoldi, Avvocato De Marchi, Nereggia, Sugarloaf Maled (the King), Rodolfo and Enzo De Mei, Nello Tommasini, Cavaliere Areni, Testaccio, Lello Raveni, Leonardo Barini, and a number of youths with big noses and hair as bristly as besoms.

Francesco Buscaino was seated towards the top end of the table, but was far from satisfied with the general attitude of the assembly. No one seemed willing to emerge entirely from the shell of his own thoughts. From time to time Buscaino had a tray passed round laden with brimming glasses, but these liqueurs caused all present to withdraw into themselves still further. Lello Raveni tipped his cigarette in the air and attempted to produce smoke-rings into which he could then poke a finger. Sometimes the ring disintegrated, at others it rose so fast that Lello had practically to leap onto his chair to get his finger through it. Rodolfo looked daggers at him, trying to make him keep still. "Hang on a mo'," said Lello abstractedly. "Just one more! The very last!" But he added almost inaudibly, "If I bring this one off I'll bring it off with Luisa." Tommasini was subjecting him to close scrutiny, especially that part of his face where the imperceptible motion of his lips was creating shadowy creases. And he thought to himself, "This young chap's worth watching. Maybe one of these days . . ."

On the other side of the table was another personage who never kept still for an instant: Testaccio, who at frequent intervals dived at his ankles as if to swat a fly, beat at them fiercely and muttered under his breath, "Inky pinky panky pox, spirits of evil leave my socks!"

The third and last fidget was provided by the index finger of Avvocato De Marchi who, here as elsewhere, was in the process of composing a waltz and beating time to it the while.

The rest of them admittedly sat still, but from time to time they were swept by a gust of meaningless laughter that seemed to split them in half as a knife splits water-melons. This thought occurred to Buscaino, to be followed immediately by a second: "My God, people like this are going to take some persuading! But persuaded they shall be!"

And he rose to his feet.

No sooner had he done so than they all turned to face him, adopting comfortable positions especially for the head, which in Natàca (another of Buscaino's observations) was in constant need of support, as if it were about to come adrift from the body. They stared at him in silence.

"Gentlemen," began Buscaino, "you are all to some extent acquainted with my project for a hundred-and-fifty-foot tower to be built on the northern side of the city, up which the Natàcans will be allowed to mount upon payment of two lire per head."

"Excuse me, professor," put in Tommasini, "but why *two* lire? Why not five?"

"Five seems to me overdoing it. Our tower must be accessible to the man in the street, the man with a slim pocket. When the beggar from Via Messina gets to the top of our tower, we shall commemorate the event with a marble plaque; for it will signify that the last drop of the city, squeezed from the very lees of it, has fallen into our wineglass."

"Excellent! Well spoken, professor!" interrupted Tommasini once again.

"Signor Tommasini, please leave applause till the end and, if you can, leave it out altogether."

"Dear professor, don't tell me you've taken it the wrong way . . ."

"Tommasini, I ask you again: let me speak! For better or for worse, let me speak!"

"Shut up, for God's sake!" roared Rodolfo. "Why is it that we can never get anything serious done here?"

"Have no fear, Rodolfo," continued Buscaino. "We are going to, and that right soon! In a word, gentlemen, my project requires an expenditure of one hundred thousand lire, which sum will be immediately indemnified by earnings of a clear six hundred thousand. I repeat: six hundred thousand lire net! I don't think that is a deal to be sneezed at. Any American, for such a deal, would put his life on the line. But I am not asking for your lives, simply for your cordial collaboration, your expeditious assistance. Rest assured. At the end of the evening I am not going to pass round a silver salver for you to stack your money on. I am *not going to ask for money!*"

"In that case, Buscaino, what are you going to ask for?" queried Enzo De Mei with furrowed brow.

"I will ask you simply for advice. And I'll start at once. What, in your opinion, is the best way of collecting the requisite sum from the citizens of your – and may I say also *my* – town?"

"May one speak?" ventured Avvocato De Marchi.

"Certainly, your Honour! We shall be happy to hear what you have to say."

"Well then, it's like this . . . In my opinion the wealthiest persons in Natàca will never be willing to rip up their floors or slit open their mattresses to disgorge the money needed to build a tower. We must obtain our funds in another way . . ."

"And that is? Say on . . ."

"Well then . . . We should put on a grandiose spectacle, if possible religious in character."

"What, process through the streets?"

"Tommasini, for God's sake shut your trap! You can have your say later. Proceed, your Honour."

"What I suggest is . . . a theatrical performance. And we have a wonderful opportunity: we have, still unpublished, my friend Nereggia's 'Santa Genoveffa', which has received the praises of the Archbishop himself; and which, in this fool of a town, has found not a blessed soul willing to stage it."

"But . . ."

"Please continue, your Honour. Pay no attention. Go on, go on."

"Santa Genoveffa is the patroness of the city. The people venerate this saint. There's no hole in the wall in which you do not find her sacred image. You should visit those streets in which the lost women lurk, the twopenny whores."

"We'll be there this evening, all together in a body."

"Will you too keep your trap shut, Enzo De Mei. You can speak later . . . Please continue, your honour."

"Well, walking along those streets and looking in at the doorways you can see rooms positively papered with pictures of Santa Genoveffa. Now I say to you: if the saint's holy image has spread so far and so wide, on the evening we give a theatrical performance bearing the very name of our patron saint, is there a soul in Natàca who would stay at home? We'll have takings of thousands upon thousands of lire! I myself will write the choral music . . . and we shall be giving pleasure to our friend Nereggia, upon whom until now Fortune has rarely smiled . . ."

Nereggia squeezed the Avvocato's arm firmly but without a word, and lowered his eyelids so as not to reveal what the eyes of a sensitive poet could achieve in a moment of gratitude.

"It's an idea, an idea!" exclaimed Buscaino. "And I have every admiration for ideas. The only thing is, your Honour, it's an idea that, before making money, requires money spent on it. And money is exactly what we haven't got."

These last words of Buscaino's acted like a cold shower. Everyone froze.

"Or rather, to put it better, we don't need to dip our hands in our pockets, in view of the fact that we have tabled a project that in itself is worth its weight in gold. Let us produce the ideas, and others produce the money. If we wanted to do the thinking and spend money at the same time, there'd be no need for us to set up a limited company. The tower would be all our own. We could call it the Buscaino Tower and it would pour all the six hundred thousand lire of its immediate earnings into our own pockets. We must therefore search for an expedient other than a costly theatrical performance."

"If that's the case," said De Marchi, already distinctly huffy, "you'll have a job to convince such skinflints as the propertied classes here in Natàca that this tower project is a serious proposition."

"A serious proposition! Your Honour, I'm astonished, I am profoundly astonished by what you say. What, I ask you – and I do not speak of serious objections, but any objection even futile, carping or merely whimsical – can be brought to bear against my project?"

"Well for one thing," said Nereggia, "that your whole project is hot air."

"Hot air, Professor Nereggia? If my project is hot air, then I myself am skating on thin ice. But why, if I may ask, is my project hot air?"

"Let me put it this way. If we build this tower we spend a hundred thousand lire. But what happens when the tower is built, the stairs all swept, the doors flung wide . . . and nobody crosses the threshold, nobody treads the stairs, nobody climbs to the top?"

"In the face of such an objection I have no choice but to make my bow, a very low bow indeed, and withdraw."

There was a moment of silence.

"Yes, gentlemen, say nothing and withdraw; say nothing, withdraw, and book a cabin on the S.S. Rex . . . Nobody climb our tower? . . . Very well, and what if the son we bring into the world were to have no hole to pee through? Extremely inconvenient, certainly. But in the business of fathering children, show me the man who has such a thought in mind! Or even if he does, does he take it into serious consideration? . . . Nobody climb the stairs! This, if you will permit me to say so, is a morbid suggestion. Why on earth *should* no one climb the stairs?"

"Well, you see, because . . . because no one might think it worth two lire to admire the panorama of Natàca."

"Ha ha, I'd have a good laugh, I'd stay awake all night to laugh twelve hours at a stretch, were it not for the fact that in spite of everything, gentlemen, you inspire in me an enormous sense of respect. So two lire is too much to view the panorama of Natàca? You willingly spend a lira to send some distant friend a postcard of the panorama of Natàca. On Wednesday market days even the poorest housewives spend three lire on a painted panorama of Natàca. And I speak of mere pictures, flat as pancakes, seen from below . . . anything but a living, throbbing, immense panorama spread at your very feet."

"It's true!" cried Rodolfo. "He's talking sense!"

"Let me put it this way. What if this tower, at the first tremor of an earthquake, were simply to collapse?"

"My dear professor, and if I tonight were to be kidnapped by three Chicago gangsters whom I'd been foolish enough to take a pot shot at? Every word you say bears witness to your particular cast of thought, strictly poetic as it is and not in the least practical. I have the greatest admiration for you as a poet, but have many reservations concerning your worth as a man of hard-headed practicality."

"You are right, perfectly right, Professor Buscaino. I speak not another word."

"Is there anyone else who would care to raise objections of a kind which we might, perhaps, call of the essence? No one? In that case I beg you to give me some practical advice. I was born here, but my upbringing was entrusted to five different tutors: Northern Europe, America, Asia, Africa and Australia. I know the nature of my countrymen, but I do not know them in person. Inform me, therefore, of the best way of persuading the richest citizens of Natàca to buy shares in our company, and what the names of the aforesaid might be."

"Can I talk?" asked Cavaliere Areni.

"Of *course* you can!" sniggered Tommasini, not willing to lose the chance of giving yet another prod to the *cavaliere*'s already wobbly wits.

"I should appreciate it if, inside the tower, there were to be a dance-hall."

"Always in the swing is our *cavaliere*!" cried Enzo De Mei, observing the old man with an expression less crafty than studious and penetrating.

"Don't worry, your Honour," said Tommasini. "The tower will work by day and have fun by night. We shall have our dance-hall. Professor Buscaino told me so himself."

"Tommasini, I never told you anything of the sort! I would ask you not to start spreading false rumours about my project. Before long they'll be saying that I came to Natàca to erect a vertical teashop!"

"But my dear professor! The idea of a dance-hall wasn't mine. It was yours!"

"Tommasini, what you say is entirely incorrect, and it's wrong of you to go on about it."

"I beg your pardon, professor, but I have to go on about it, because I remember word for word your conversation with me about the need for a dance-hall on the second floor of the tower."

"I swear that yesterday I had no conversation with you."

"Well that's very odd . . . very odd indeed . . . It was quite a long speech you made."

"Are you being serious?"

"On my honour!"

"I entirely fail to understand you. How can I have said such a thing, when the idea of a second-floor dance-hall has not so much as crossed my mind? And how can I have done so yesterday, seeing that we didn't even meet?"

"Didn't even meet? My dear professor, I begin to feel concerned for you. We spent two hours together. You stood me a cherry brandy, then bought an American book and said, 'I'll be getting back to the hotel to read a bit of this play I've heard so much about.'"

"An American book? A play? . . . Tommasini, would you mind stepping this way for a moment?"

He led Tommasini to a corner of the room, and in a voice which, though low, was not a little angry, "Tommasini," he said, "what exactly are you playing at? I can see straight through you! Had I wished to go mad, there've been more likely times than this. There in America, during a brief but bleak period of my life, when I worked in the mines and went about the streets down and out, times when the black man working behind you spits his quid onto your back, or an urchin in the streets sets his dog on you, what better time to cry out 'I want the sun!' or 'I am the king of France!'? But here, and at your hands, no thanks! Give it up, Tommasini. I have no intention of going mad and enhancing the museum of your victims!"

Tommasini bestowed upon him a look of deep affection which seemed to say, "Why do you work so hard? Why tire yourself out? My dear professor, put your trust in me. It's not a matter of going mad, as you put it, but merely of relaxing." And indeed in that lad's eyes there was a gleam as of a serene and tranquil harbour in which to drop anchor after a long and troubled voyage. Buscaino waggled his hand before his eyes as if to wave something away, and added, "Tommasini, let us stay on friendly terms. Just drop your schemings as far as I am concerned, and give me some real help. You follow me? Let us now resume our seats."

Back at the table, having given his lips a mop with a silk handkerchief, Buscaino recommenced as follows:

"I should now like to hear from the young people who are the very backbone of any enterprise, and are not mealy-mouthed. You, Lello Raveni, instead of filling the room with smoke-rings, speak up! Your father is a wealthy landowner. Do you think he might be willing to be a founder member of The Panoramic Tower Company?"

Buscaino was at this point hurriedly approached by Rodolfo, who whispered in his ear: "I ought to tell you that only this morning Signor Raveni discovered a note from Luisa the chambermaid in one of his son's socks. All hell broke loose!"

"I understand," said Buscaino quietly. "Indeed I understand. Delicate matters. I say no more."

Lello Raveni, having read on Rodolfo's lips the precise words which had set them in motion, thought upon the *billet-doux* he had in his pocket: "Lello, soul of my life, my hope to all eternity, have no fear, we shall win through," and his mind wandered so far from the room that he instantly forgot Buscaino's question, and indeed his very existence.

The latter now addressed Leonardo: "And has Signor Leonardo Barini nothing to say to us?"

Leonardo, his head reclining on the back of his chair, had his eyes on the ceiling where Lello's smoke-rings were vanishing, pondering on everything he had heard said, and wondering why the earth should be burdened with a scene such as this, and what the mysterious intentions of destiny could be. Finally he rose to his feet and laughed.

This laugh might have been a bell ringing for the end of a boring and tiresome lesson. Everyone stood up, with good-natured merriment, as if the joke was over and about time too, because they had quite sufficiently committed themselves.

Buscaino did not know how to prevent these people from so boorishly eluding him. "Well then?" he demanded. "Are we, or are we not, proposing to proceed with this discussion? Or shall we postpone it until tomorrow?"

Rodolfo replied to this by giving him a good poke in the ribs and saying, "You rogue! You rascal you!"

"Shall we make it tomorrow? Or the next day?"

"Or the next blue moon," muttered De Marchi, thrusting his arms into his black greatcoat very markedly.

The gnat of a man Nereggia wrapped himself entirely round and about in a pea-green mack and, from its innards, interspersed with gusts of laughter, ejaculated sounds such as "Ha ha . . . yes yes . . . this tower . . . ha ha . . . Oh yes, oh no . . . ha ha ha . . ."

Tommasini sidled up to Buscaino and suggested in an undertone, "I think it's time for us to leave. Later, we'll see. In any case, I'll stick by you. Enzo De Mei backs me up."

Once out in the street, however, not a soul kept faith with Buscaino.

From his second-floor room he was obliged to overhear much loud and boisterous laughter, the word "tower" uttered in a most derisory manner, and eventually the noises people make when they turn to fisticuffs out of sheer hilarity, shoving each other against the steel shutters of the shop-fronts, which responded with a hollow, mournful booming.

"Damn it!" thought Buscaino. "I'm going to win this one! They've simply *got* to come along with me. They're straws in the wind, but I am the wind itself and will make them whirl. I must be patient, and dedicate a little while to this."

III

How was it that things begun under such unfavourable auspices came to take a turn for the better? Many indeed were the reasons, but paramount among them was the conduct of Francesco Buscaino.

Following that ill-starred meeting in the hotel lounge, at which we were present, Buscaino showed no sign of flying off the handle; nor did he retain a jot of resentment against those who had filled the street beneath the hotel windows with clamour and guffaws; nor did his face betray aught but its habitual leanness . . . And – most worthy of note – he did not leave Natàca.

Elegantly swathed in his long green topcoat, he spent hour after hour in the cafés, speaking in the most urbane manner conceivable, frequently addressing the humbler auditor rather than the more classy one, and an acquaintance met that moment rather than a friend of some standing, and narrating some of the events in his life, though more to pass the time than to talk about himself. Prefacing his remark with "a trifle", or "a mere nothing, just the follies of youth, you know", he disclosed the fact that Bulù, captain of the Moorish pirates, had once given him a ring encrusted with diamonds. He then hastily passed on to further episodes, so as to speak of Bulù rather than of himself. To the diminutive fellows who were listening with looks of dismay and envy, occasionally getting up from the table to rise on tiptoe, then rock back on their heels, he would say: "Do you imagine that Bulù is a giant? Think nothing of the sort! Bulù is round about my own build, and weighs fifty kilos, if that! In your company he would seem a mere stripling!"

Maria Careni's wedding, which took place around that time, was attended by Buscaino in the smartest morning coat ever seen in Natàca. He proposed a toast destined to remain in the memories of the guests for a long time to come: "Ladies and gentlemen," he said, "I have this day achieved I will not tell you how many years, but they are many. Yes, I have achieved . . . In a word, each time the month of March comes round, the day on which I had the honour to be born (an honour which you, sweet bride, will shortly confer on beings far worthier than I), each time, I say, on each recurrence of the date on which I was born, God grants that I be present at something grand and special. Thus on one occasion, upon my birthday, I was privileged to be present at the first wireless transmission, accomplished by Guglielmo Marconi. This year destiny permits me to attend your wedding. I am going from strength to strength . . ."

And that was merely the preamble.

One afternoon, seeing the good results obtained during an hour which – having nothing better to do – he had spent tracing the outlines of certain coloured illustrations, it occurred to him to put on a one-man show in a small room in the hotel. "Mere nothings!" he said. "The lines are few, but essential."

Many were the visitors, among them the crusty old Professor Laveni, who talked like a book of ancient chronicles, bunching his huge fists every time he came out with a term such as embrasure, architrave, ovolo, sconce or opisthodomos. "Now then," said the professor, while his voice, despite all his efforts to keep it low, soared ever higher until the notes became a screech, and he was in a cold sweat, like one attempting to pull down a balloon and hanging more and more desperately onto the string which is bearing him skywards: "Now then, my dear Buscaino, you can't deceive me! You have devoted long study to our sixteenth-century painters."

"Heavens alive," replied Buscaino quietly, "I've spent *years* in the Uffizi."

This episode, together with a host of others, such as hastening to buy a coffee for complete strangers who were patting their pockets in the vain hope of locating a wallet; such as rummaging for a photograph and inadvertently letting fall a thousand-lire note which he then picked up with neither hurry nor concern; such as never mentioning the tower except by vague allusions to projects which look absurd on the surface but in fact are goldmines. These things made Buscaino the most talked-about figure in Natàca. He was laughed at occasionally, but this kind of mirth was unique to Natàca and had nothing spiteful about it. It was like a compulsive yawn that gives no offence to a lecturer, because it means not that the yawner is bored, but simply that for reasons extraneous to the excellent lecture he is out of sorts.

In the meantime Rodolfo and Leonardo, meeting (as they did every evening) in Giovanni Luisi's dining-room, devoted many a long hour to the tower scheme. Giovanni's Uncle Roberto would listen to these discussions with a smile more rubicund than ever, as if the glad, mysterious events which had for years been happening in his person had found an opportunity for becoming even more mysterious and glad.

"In short," said Rodolfo, "this project is not entirely unserious. The trouble is that when anyone comes up with anything new here in Natàca, the first thing people do is look for a reason to laugh at it. But what's so laughable about a panoramic tower? Practically all towns have some sort of high point where you can go and look at what they call a fine view. In my opinion there's work to be done on this project, and not for nothing either. There's a chance of making some money."

"You know what?" said Leonardo, "I don't have much faith in what this tower might earn in the future. But I'm beginning to think that a scheme of this sort, with lots of work and lots of worries, is what we need to occupy our lives. Unfortunately, the vacuum in our lives is so big that there's plenty of room in them for a hundred-and-fifty-foot tower."

Giovanni Luisi regarded his friends, sometimes severely, sometimes with a childlike smile, the latter conveying that the building of this tower was the best idea in the world, the former that it was a rotten one and its promoter an adventurer.

"An adventurer!" murmured Leonardo. "So much the better. If Buscaino is really an adventurer he'll have a colossal success in Natàca. In a town like this, full of poor creeps who can't tear themselves away from their own firesides, an adventurer is like a libertine from the big city arriving at some lonely house inhabited by romantically-minded spinsters. Daring, unscrupulous men wipe the floor with respectable loafers."

The walls of Casa Luisi were not the only ones eavesdropping on such discussions. Whether for him or against, Buscaino was the talk of the town. One day Testaccio, as he stood at the counter in a café, said that the serene spirits had informed him that the tower project was well thought-of in the upper regions of the heavens. Everyone laughed. But then Leopoldi, playing at Lotto, selected the symbols Tower, Sky and Madman, and won the jackpot. This win set Natàca buzzing. That very Saturday afternoon a Milanese architect, yawning away after a lunch that had brought to his stomach much what flood waters bring to the sea – every sort of dead meat and veg. – leant an elbow on the table and, resting his head on his hand, exclaimed, "This project you mention seems to me a bright idea. It could well be profitable, in my opinion."

By sheer coincidence, at that very moment Buscaino said to Rodolfo, "My dear De Mei, you are a man after my own heart. You need to be on the move to stay alive. Now, if instead of running up and down the stairs of the lawcourts where, not being a lawyer, you have no business; if instead of making footling telephone calls in the middle of the night to people you scarcely know, and dashing off on a motorbike to villages where, indeed, a new house could well be built, but where no one has asked you to design I do not say a house, but so much as a hovel; if instead of all this you come and work with me, be my support, and employ all the artfulness of your charm to persuade the most affluent citizens of Natàca to relinquish their avarice, and then design a tower which will *really be built* . . .

Well don't you think, De Mei, that you would be raising your life, lock, stock and barrel, to a somewhat higher plane?"

Rodolfo gave him a smile such as a lover might bestow on a loved-one, not wishing to betray by one iota the new emotion boiling in his breast.

"Furthermore," continued Buscaino, "Natàca has never shown itself averse to schemes involving risks and sacrifices. Here it was that they chose to try out the machine for producing artificial rain. The water, alas, extracted from sandy soil, proved salt, and the project was a flop. But in this very town they are plotting to stage a *coup de main* in the Republic of San Marino. It is here, moreover, that Leopoldi has discovered perpetual motion and Neri invented Morreale. The spirit of initiative is by no means lacking in Natàca. It is simply that up to now it has been poorly managed and directed. Now, I shouldn't like to think that at the very moment when fortune sends you a good manager (because, when you come down to it, my scheme is well thought-out, and no one has been able to raise any but the most puerile objections to it); I repeat, I should not like to think that this spirit of initiative could so crassly throw away the chance of being properly directed towards its goal. What do you think?"

"Perhaps . . ." murmured Rodolfo, "perhaps you are right. In fact, there's no doubt about it!"

"Buscaino is right. There's no doubt about it!" These were the words that, in a flash, took the best part of Natàca by storm. Yes, a tower a hundred and fifty foot high. That's something, now! That little chap's brains must reach all the way down to his toenails. A tower with a dance-hall on the second floor, in fact *two* of them! With a telescope, with a silver screen, with a huge clock, with a cannon to blast off at midday, with a lighthouse, with a cage and an eagle flapping its wings in it, with a hat shop, a hotel, a gaming den, an altar to say Mass at, a fencing school, a small bazaar – in short something that will be a lasting memorial to the work put in on this project by the particular citizen of Natàca who is at the moment expounding and lauding it. Yea, a tower we say! A tower!

"When we're rich," said Rodolfo to Leonardo, "we'll be off to Rome. You said one evening that what we needed to make us happy was a job to work on together, one that would unite all our efforts. Well, this might be what we've been waiting for, don't you think?"

"Maybe," murmured Leonardo, massaging his grey-matter gently with one hand. "No, not maybe! Definitely! The days won't be so wearisome, and what's more we'll earn a lot of money. All the same, from time to time I really do think I've gone round the bend. But who cares? I may be wrong . . . in fact of course I'm wrong. So, the tower! A champion idea! Let's build the tower . . . Once I tried to write a novel. Professor Luigini gave me some hints: 'Chuck in a few characters, a smattering of a plot, a spot of real life and a bit of feeling to go along with it, and you'll write a fine novel!' But when I chuck in the characters I lose touch with the truth, and when I bung in the feeling the plot goes to pieces. Better to leave novel-writing alone. Anyway, everything around me is still pitch-black. Ever since I got back to Natàca it seems to have been always night: from that day to this has been nothing but a night, one single, unending night. Will I ever see the sun again? Yes, I believe I will. But in the meantime, seeing as it's night, and I may well be dreaming, there's nothing in the least odd about building a tower, and nothing odd in the idea that this might be the most serious thing one could possibly do."

"You're raving!"

"Not at all. I'll join in and get to work. At once. It's quite right, what Buscaino said: we have to get together an executive committee. You, your brother, Tommasini and Buscaino. A group of people with their wits about them who will visit the bigwigs of Natàca and immediately come up with the support we need."

"You think so?"

"I'm sure of it."

★

"Yes!" agreed Buscaino. "An executive committee! We'll get down to it at once. There are three persons on whom we have to go to work and ripen their sensibilities . . . They are, unfortunately, three highly acidulous old fruits. But we shall get the better of them. The first, my dear Rodolfo, is your affluent client Duke Fausto Villadora; the second is that celebrated professor of international law, Federico Solco; while the third is Cavaliere De Filippi, the dialect poet. Yes, because here in Natàca the money is in the hands of dialect poets . . . We'll begin with him. But while I think of it, Giovanni Luisi is worrying me not a little. The land on which we are going to have to build belongs to his mother. When I learnt that I felt as happy as a sandboy. But then I thought again. That lad is a member of our Organizing Committee, but has he ever attended a meeting? Has he ever said a word in our support?"

"Don't worry. He will!" said Rodolfo.

"He will! He will! I don't like this future tense. It implies uncertainty and waste of time. I make a point of saving even minutes, and am miserly in spending my time, Rodolfo. Here, on the other hand, you squander it. We must change the whole system!"

Rodolfo grinned. "We are at your service," he said.

"That Giovanni Luisi, now. Every few seconds he changes his mind. At one moment he says yes, and at the next he's saying 'Didn't you hear me? I said no!' I'm inclined to think that he's never kept a single appointment. After lunch sleep throws a halter round his neck and leads him – come hell or high water – off to his bedroom."

"Actually, he's a good lad."

"Right! Because to be really nasty you have to have a spirit of initiative. And of that spirit he has not a jot or a tittle."

"Listen Francesco, if you've come here to cast aspersions on my friends . . ."

"Your friends are my friends, and I have every right to train them up and alter them for the better. A good lad! It strikes me that for some time now he's even been getting a bit above himself. If you say to him, 'You know, Dante used to have a good snooze after lunch,' he won't come back with 'Ah, I am like Dante!' On the contrary, he'll say, 'I'm glad to hear it. Dante was like me!' Dante like him, indeed! And then he goes out of his way to humiliate poor Leonardo, who is no Dante but at least knows how to hold a pen. Leonardo, for his part, looks to me like a fly, *une mouche*, that has been half squashed and wants nothing better than to get squashed altogether. He too has his shortcomings, with that woebegone childish expression, as though someone for a lark had popped him on top of a chest of drawers, and instead of trying to climb down or yelling for help, he sits there brooding on his fate as a woebegone child left sitting on a chest of drawers."

"Oh, Francesco, don't go on like that! Why don't we go and see Giovanni at once? It's Sunday, and he'll be alone in the house. We'll be free to talk."

"Splendid idea! I wish for nothing better. But there's one thing, Rodolfo. It's four o'clock. I have to get away at five — I've got an appointment. I'm a stickler about appointments."

"You'll get away, don't worry."

"Right you are then."

Giovanni Luisi is thirty-five and has never done a hand's turn, or written a line. He is now in bed, neither reading nor thinking, but staring at the bedside lamp and fiddling with the wire of the electric bell. Nevertheless, most prominent in his bosom at this time is a feeling of pride. He is perfectly pleased with himself, and sincerely believes that he is a man of exceptional merit. The fact that he hasn't written a word is tantamount to his having written a bit of every masterpiece in the world, and never having turned his hand to anything means he has never failed in any enterprise. Whenever he thinks over his past he never ceases to find conspicuous signs of the youth of a great man: the precocity of certain feelings; a fortune-teller who discovered such signs in his palm that they made her jump out of her skin; the desire to be alone. And that contempt for other people, that onrush of love for every one of them, the absolute requirement *not* to see them, and the pleasure of their company. Even now, for example, is he not the spitting image of that impetuous, fickle Peer Gynt, who flirted with every form that life could take, and would leave a woman for a lofty tree, and that lofty tree for a shapely boat? Is he not like him in this sudden love-affair with the electric bell, and not noticing that the doorbell has been ringing for half an hour, and that someone, perhaps a friend, is waiting at the door? Yes, he's fond enough of his friends, but is it maybe not noble and spiritual to neglect them once in a while to flirt with a poor inanimate wire, grey, what is more, and disregarded by all? *That* is what is missing in the world today: greatness of soul, fullness of heart. Writers are imbeciles. Your Leonardo is a miserable, dry stick of an intellectual who hasn't the guts to get himself recognized by the confraternity of inanimate objects and living beings as what in fact a writer ought to be: their relative, their brother.

The bell's ringing, but who cares? Giovanni picks up the book which has fallen face down on the floor and re-reads the page he has marked in pencil. Ah ha, this page says exactly what he was saying to himself a moment ago. One really doesn't have to read books, especially great ones: they say nothing but what one has already thought of oneself . . . So let the damned bell ring to its heart's content!

In the meantime, outside the door, "Jesus, Mary and Joseph!" stormed Buscaino. "We've been ringing for half an hour. This lad is driving me nuts!"

"He wasn't always like this," said Rodolfo.

"You're *all* like this in Natàca! . . . But come what may I am not standing here a moment longer. I have to go! But I ask you, Rodolfo, if we waste so much time on the simplest things, the mere preliminaries, where are we likely to end up? I'm in a hurry. I have to get back to America. I've got a fiancée waiting for me, for God's sake! Either these men are prepared to keep pace with me or I shall abandon the lot of them to the catafalques of their mattresses! Farewell to you!"

IV

THE EXECUTIVE COMMITTEE climbed the main staircase towards the De Filippi apartment. In the van went Buscaino, shaking his head gently from side to side and every so often waving a hand as if to ward off someone approaching him too closely. Behind him came Rodolfo and Enzo De Mei, and Nello Tommasini.

Buscaino swivelled on his heels and stopped to face his friends from the step above. "Signora Luisi," he said, "has at last conceded us the land on which to build the tower. But it has taken a whole month! All the fault of that blessèd son of hers who now – mark my words! – only now has taken our project seriously and is as proud of it as if he had thought of it himself. He does not say 'Buscaino's tower,' but 'My tower'. However, I complain not about that, but only because we've lost a month. And we have not yet confronted the major part of the problem. The hard part begins today. I beg you, friends, to applaud and compliment our dialect poet at every opportunity. I think of you as vessels overflowing with 'well dones' and 'well said sirs'. Pour them out with moderation at the beginning, but at the end with vehemence!

"In America now, a project like mine is not negotiated in this manner. It is enough to expound it for cash to come floating down like doves to scattered grain. Here we are forced to listen to poetry, to cope with Giovanni Luisi's slumbers, and God knows what else! My wife, poor dear . . ."

"Have you *got* a wife?" queried Rodolfo.

"Of course I have. Why not?"

"Well . . . where is she?"

"In America, of course."

"You're a married man!" stammered Enzo De Mei.

"Enzo, dear boy, I don't care for this tone of voice. Everything that comes out of your mouth sounds like a translation of such a phrase as 'it's the end of the world and we are all lost.' Come off it. Get a bit of the spice of life into you! And don't go on nosing around lunatics, because loonies aren't what makes things tick . . . And Tommasini, watch yourself! Don't, for the love of God, take it into your head to send Cavaliere De Filippi off his rocker. Be serious, and for once in your life resign yourself to leaving a man in the mental condition which God has given him."

Having so said, he climbed the last few steps, arrived at the door and tugged at the bell-rope. Without, however, eliciting a sound from the bell.

"I see!" exclaimed Buscaino. "It's the usual bit of string attached to a dried tomato. O my fist, turn thou to stone!" And he began to hammer his clenched fist upon the resounding drumhead of the door.

"I'm coming, I'm coming," cried a woman's voice. "Give me time, for pity's sake! Who's there?"

"Friends."

"Signora, there's honest folk at the door. Shall I let 'em in?"

"Ask 'em who they are!" cried another and more distant voice.

"Who are you?"

"My good woman, we are friends of the *cavaliere*'s."

A shuffling of footsteps was heard, then a creaking of rusty hinges, and high up in the wall there opened a hidden little window, and a crumpled old face filled it. The eyes in this face began laboriously to scrutinize Buscaino, who was revolving slowly and obligingly as a fashion model: "Have you observed, granny, that we are gentlemen? Your master is expecting us . . ."

"Indubitably!" a voice was heard at this point to declare on the other side of the door, amid the rasping of bolts and removal of bars. "Indubitably! My good friend Professor Buscaino!"

The door swung wide and on the threshold appeared a little old man in evening dress, as if he were a visitor in his own house. He even had his hat on, the brim on one side tilted in youthful fashion almost down to his nose, while beneath the turned up portion appeared a merry eye, though the pupil was white.

"Here, professor, an embrace!" said the old man opening his arms. "I've been expecting you for an hour."

Buscaino introduced himself gradually into the arms of the *cavaliere* while courteously pressing his own against those skimpy, black-clad shoulders. "These are my friends," he said. "Rodolfo De Mei, the architect, his brother Signor Enzo De Mei, and Signor Tommasini."

"Splendid, gentlemen! Come along in! Do, please, keep your hats on. It's cold in here. I always wear a hat, as you can see."

"But that cannot be, my dear *Cavaliere*! After all, we are in the house of Poesy!"

"Very well then, you force me to go bare-headed." And so saying their host swept off his hat, revealing a cranium so pointed and repellent that the four friends deemed it wiser to conceal that sight by keeping their own hats on.

"Excellent, excellent! Come along into the drawing-room. I will present you to my dear wife. We're always bickering, the old girl and I, but we are fond of each other all the same. And you, dear professor, must try to persuade her that the time I devote to the Muses of the local tongue are by no means wasted hours!"

"Of course, of course. I shall certainly win her round. Have no fear but I shall persuade your good lady!"

"Have a care not to get all dusty. This passage is where I keep all my grandfather's sticks of furniture. Sometimes I think of burning them. But then again, they have so many memories for me. The chair there on your right, which no longer bears any resemblance to a chair, for twenty years – and I say twenty years! – sustained and supported a poor uncle of mine who was afraid to stand on his feet."

"Good one!" murmured Enzo De Mei with genuine admiration. "And why was he afraid?"

"Because he thought that if he stood up the tiny amount of blood left in his body would all sink down to his knees, leaving his brain exposed to the danger of cooling down once and for all."

"Is your uncle dead?" enquired Enzo with considerable interest.

"Of course, of course. Years ago. But here we are . . ."

And arriving at a small door he made way for his visitors to enter. "Thank you, thank you," said they, emerging into an enormous drawing-room in which a cold hearth seemed to put an even intenser chill into the already frigid air. The ceiling was exceedingly high, and shrouded in darkness. The frescos on the walls, through their overall tone of slate-grey, revealed an occasional blood-stained foot or green head bowled far from its body. The windows, masked by curtains of dark purple, cast spiders'-webs of light which attached themselves here to the flooring, there to the backs of a number of upholstered chairs dotted about at random in the middle of the room.

"Maria!" commanded the *cavaliere*. "Switch on the light!"

"Switch it on yourself! You're right next to it!" replied a woman's voice from one of the chairs in the centre of the room.

"God give me patience! Don't ever think of getting married, my friends . . . However, let us turn on the light."

An enormous wrought-iron chandelier shed harsh beams floorwards. The first thing they fell upon was something white, thick and bulky, placed upon a table, which the visitors were quick to recognize as a manuscript. A yard or so from the table a minuscule woman, black-clad and seated in a chair so high that it left dangling in space two feet encased in old-fashioned shoes extending so far above the ankle as to vanish beneath her skirts like boots, and fastened (after a fashion) with a double row of buttons, ceased clicking her knitting-needles and blinked her eyes a few times at the sudden bright light, with the air of a rabbit sniffing at a lettuce leaf.

"My wife," said the *cavaliere*, indicating the old lady who was still hard-pressed to keep her eyes open. "This, Maria, is Professor Buscaino, over from America."

The tiny lady slid down from her chair and offered her visitors a hand that was infinitesimal in size, cold on one side and hot on the other, extremely feeble on both sides, and with something in the middle of the palm which felt like a piece of sandpaper.

"Coffee!" commanded the *cavaliere*. "Quick about it, Donna Maria: fetch the coffee."

"Dammit!" exclaimed Donna Maria. "I thought of it earlier. It won't take a minute."

V

When his wife had left the room, the *cavaliere* seated his four visitors in a semicircle and took his place behind the manuscript.

"Gentlemen," he said, "I will not stand upon ceremony. I shall begin to read at once. These are simple little things, just as they spring from the heart, and written in the language we learnt at our mother's knee."

Buscaino emitted a few dry coughs, lowered his hat-brim over his eyes, inserted his hands into his sleeves and curled up like a cat before the fire.

"These are poems written with the soul of a peasant. For when it comes down to it I am a man as simple and natural as the grass that grows. I swear to you that sometimes, as I lie beneath a tree, I relapse into a state of such utter simplicity that the bird hopping about at my side must surely have the glance of a professor compared with what I feel to be in my own eyes! In these scraps of poetry I am imagining that the vast issues which weary mankind are seen by a peasant, by a poor blockhead, and are sung in a simple, unaffected style . . ."

At this point his wife re-entered with a large tray.

"Starting already!" she muttered to her husband. "You might at least have waited for these gentlemen to have their coffee. It wouldn't have been the end of the world, dammit!"

"Madam," said Buscaino, "to imbibe a cup of coffee which – to judge from the aroma – will be most excellent, and to listen to poems which, from what I have heard, will be sublime, is a pleasure the Americans would term providential."

"D'you hear that?" demanded the *cavaliere*. "People in town are speaking well of my poetry!"

"Speaking *well!*" retorted Buscaino. "To say 'well' is saying little. They speak of it with fervour!"

His wife shrugged, and placed in Buscaino's hands a large cup brim-full of coffee.

"Maria, sit down and let me read."

"I'm sitting down, dammit!"

In a voice that all of a sudden turned reedy, as if the *cavaliere* had relinquished the floor to some tiny child hidden in his bosom, he very slowly declaimed nine sonnets and fifteen ballads in *ottava rima*. These whole-heartedly celebrated what your peasant thinks about the moon and the stars, the Copernican system as opposed to the Ptolemaic, the theories of Plato, the monads of Leibniz, the Kantian concept of space and time, Einstein's theory of relativity, the nature of intuition as preached by Bergson, of technocracy, electrons and ions, vitamins, estate management, the Quantum theory, the deterioration of matter, Theosophy, hormones, the machines which have replaced both men and animals . . . A peasant tells how his ox, looking at a small tractor, thought (needless to say in dialect): "Yes, little man, go on and drive your machine. But what, after all, *is* a machine? It is the heating up and subsequent cooling off and, if we may so put it, crystallization of the spirit. What you are driving is not a machine, but a part of your soul that is dead for ever and ever." In a word, the ox was watching the horrendous spectacle of a man riding astride his own dead soul.

Then there was another peasant who sang to his bride, "My dear, at one time there was such a thing as love, trala-trala; but now all hearts are colder than ice, trala-trala; once you would have sought in me the infinite, trala-tralee; but now in me you seek the finite, trala-tralee . . ." Then again a small boy, a shepherd's son, woke at dead of night and cried out to his mother, "Why did your lullaby sing of how lovely it is to lie down and rest? Mother dear, do me the favour of not using euphemisms (he actually said that: euphemisms), and candidly state that it is beautiful to die . . ." An old farm-hand, testing the edge of the blade of his mattock, thought: "The line between to be or not to be is finer than this mattock's edge! Ah, there is more philosophy in my mattock than in Plato's *Protagoras*!" And then again, a beggar squatting in the corner of a courtyard muttered that it was better to express oneself by metonymy than by synecdoche. In the ballads there was even a sprinkling of French words, though adapted to the phonetics of our local dialect, whereas in the sonnets the words were all impeccably dialectal, the rhymes crashed in at the end of the lines as do orchestral cymbals at the imperious sign of the conductor's baton. As he read, the *cavaliere* warmed to it like a white-hot horseshoe on which, however, fell the severe gaze of his wife, like water restoring it to blackness and hardness. But eventually the inner fervour was such that that hostile gaze had no more power over the figure of the *cavaliere*, now totally contorted and glowing red.

"Good, good, good!" exclaimed Buscaino. "I shall never cease to cry 'good, good!'. If you do not in person oblige me to desist I shall cry 'good!' and 'good for you!' until tomorrow morning . . ."

"Excellent!" cried Tommasini. "*Cavaliere*, I wonder you don't recite these lines at the Rossini Hospital."

"At the Rossini Hospital?" queried the *cavaliere* in a far-away voice.

"Just so. My uncle runs the hospital. He would be happy to present his patients with an hour of delight such as you have bestowed on us this evening."

In vain did Buscaino, with two dry coughs and a swift kick, attempt to silence Tommasini. "Pay no attention, *Cavaliere*," he said. "Or rather, that is something we might consider at a later stage. Tommasini, I beg you do not make plans! There is no room for your plans when my own are in the offing!"

"Do you have plans?" enquired the *cavaliere*, directing his white pupil ceilingwards.

"My dear *Cavaliere*, your lines are as music to me, and music has its drawbacks: it inspires a simple man of action such as I. As I listened to your words I conceived an idea which, needless to say, has become part of my design for the tower . . . For nowadays if you split my head in half you will find a tower, if you rend my breast asunder you will find a tower, and even in the most minuscule bone of my little finger you will find a tower. It is what you might call a fixation which I cannot rid myself of, but which in my view does me no dishonour. In New York, where I was a well-known figure, my friends used to ask me, 'Mr Buscaino, what's your fixation for today?' On one occasion I hoisted up the sole of my shoe and showed them a thumb-tack that had gotten fixed in there. 'That's it,' said I."

Enzo De Mei burst into a fit of laughter so loud and so sudden that Signora De Filippi was swept along by it like a hen carried away by flood waters, giving an embrarrassed little cackle. Nor did the rest of them remain indifferent to the thunderclap that boomed from the young man's lungs and bent him double. Buscaino was on the point of feeling truly flattered by it when Enzo, wiping the tears from his eyes and brushing his hair off his forehead, explained that he hadn't laughed at the thumb-tack story at all, but simply because he happened to be in a good mood that day, and that everything seemed to him so very pleasant, especially the quiet entering at the windows, and this type of room with its lofty ceiling. In particular he had laughed because it had been suddenly borne in on him that poor loonies were not mental deficients but jesters who at a certain point in their lives had sat back on their haunches like donkeys and refused to budge, had remained fixed, *fixated*.

"How on earth," said Buscaino, not a little crestfallen, "did you manage to think up all this while I was telling my thumb-tack story?"

"Well," answered De Mei, as his laughter began again, deep in his chest like the undertow on a stormy beach, "it may have been because of that thumbtack fixed in your shoe. You know what I mean . . . getting fixed . . . getting fixated on something . . ."

"Oh quite, quite."

"However, Professor Buscaino," interjected De Filippi, clasping his hands on the manuscript, "would you not care to elucidate this idea of yours?"

"No sooner said than done. On the second storey of the tower there will be something which will give you a very great deal of pleasure."

"What?" asked the *cavaliere* with eagerness.

"A lecture room. You see what I mean? We shall have poetry readings. A loudspeaker, placed on the balcony, will make the words audible outside."

"And who is going to read this poetry?"

"*Cavaliere, Cavaliere*! What an innocent you are! *How* you do appeal to me . . . Who will read this poetry? Do I have to tell you?"

"Don't you understand yet?" said the lady to her husband. "*You*'ll do the reading. You'll be the Punch and Judy show of the whole town!"

"Why do you say that, madam?" said Buscaino. "You're quite wrong, I assure you."

"Well spoken, professor! Do convince her, once and for all, that being the author of dialect poems is no disgrace to a man of good breeding."

"Disgrace? Far from it! Tell me madam, do you love the saints?"

"Saints? You mean the saints in heaven?"

"The very ones, my dear lady."

"What a pagan you are! Holy mother of God! Don't you know that the saints are not loved, they are venerated?"

"Well said, madam. And what do you find in churches to honour the saints?"

The old lady knitted her brow and gave Buscaino a suspicious look. Then her brow cleared and she said: "The church, of course."

"Very well, very well, but inside, inside the church?"

"Altars."

"And then?"

"The organ."

"And then?"

"Pictures."

"And then again, in niches in the walls?"

"Statues."

"Perfectly correct: statues. So to the saints, who are let us not say merely respectable people, but venerable, men raise statues. And what do men raise to poets, after, of course, their demise? Why, statues, dear lady! It therefore follows that poets are honoured by mankind as much as saints are."

"Holy Mother of God! Poets like saints? Holy Mother of God!" She turned this way and that on her chair, casting malicious glances at Buscaino's feet and muttering incomprehensible words. Then she raised her eyes and with an expression of agony, as of one who has fallen into a trap and is getting no help from the Almighty, she said, "Poets! Very well then, poets! But proper ones!"

"And who, dear lady, are these proper poets?"

"Why, the ones who write in Italian. Dante Alighieri."

"Dante? But, dear lady, Dante wrote in the vernacular."

"In the vernacular?" exclaimed the woman, more tetchy and suspicious than ever.

"Certainly, my dear lady. In those days everyone used to write and talk in Latin. But Dante, just like your noble husband today, put his foot down and wrote in the vernacular."

"Do you hear?" exclaimed the *cavaliere*, for an instant raising the brim of his hat and revealing his other eye, the one with the dark pupil, full of satisfaction and twinkling like a star. "Do you hear?"

"So how is it," cried the poor woman, getting really ratty, "that everybody speaks Italian and not Latin?"

"Because Dante won his battle, dear lady. Because he wrote so well in the vernacular that everybody said 'Come on now, this vernacular is far better than Latin, so let's all speak vernacular.' And from then on it became the official language. In the same way, at some future date, if the *cavaliere* manages to express himself in our own dialect as well as Dante did in his, then this dialect might become the language of the entire Peninsula, and we shall hear Bills debated in Parliament in the dialect of Natàca."

"Isn't that going rather far?" asked the *cavaliere*, in ecstasy.

"Far and away too far!" shrieked his lady wife, outraged by Buscaino's logic as by some brutish assault. "Dammit, what d'you think you're saying? Dialect, vernacular, Latinus latinorum! Dammit, dammit!"

And there she sat in her chair, even tinier than before, clenching her fist and punching her lip up against her nose and looking daggers all round.

"Very well then," she said to her husband at last. "They can erect a hundred statues to you once you're dead, but I won't give you a red cent to print that horrid book of yours."

And having thus unburdened herself, she left the room.

"Christ alive!" thought Buscaino. "What's going on here? So *she*'s the one who forks out the dough . . ."

The *cavaliere* approached Buscaino and planted his hands on his shoulders. "Pay no attention, professor," he said. "Please forgive her."

"But I had no idea that your wife had the . . . that she might not allow . . . in short that your wife's position was such that . . ."

These truncated, meaningless utterances rattled the old *cavaliere*. He gave assurances that in any case his wife would soon simmer down and come out with the cash not only for that blessed book but also for the tower, the well-beloved tower which the *cavaliere* now cared for as he would for an adopted son.

"Professor Buscaino, by all means come twice a week and bring your distinguished friends if they are so minded, to listen to a brief poetry-reading, and give me your invaluable advice without reserve, and little by little get into my wife's good graces. Then, after a month or so, we'll see . . ."

So saying, the *cavaliere* darted a glance towards the part of the house whereto his wife had retreated and whither his very being cried out for him to rush, despite the apparent calm with which he accompanied (or rather, shoved) his guests along the dingy corridor and to the front door.

"A month!" cried Buscaino, as he stopped on the second landing. "Did you hear that? A whole month! Just as if he were saying half-an-hour! What do they think life is, down in these parts? Where's Tommasini?"

"He's still talking to the *cavaliere* . . . I think they're hugging one another," said Rodolfo, with a swift glance up the staircase.

"Just as long as that lad doesn't do me the dirty . . . A month, a month! . . . Ancient dotards coming apart at the seams and worn to a frazzle! I'd never dare to lay a finger on any one of them for fear he'd crumble to dust. But they've got to wake up, my dear Rodolfo! They've got to get going, even if we have to kick them in the seat of the pants. Tomorrow we are going to visit Professor Federico Solco, and this time I've got to be the winner, Christ alive!"

VI

"FRAUDULENT, delinquent, shameless, blackguardly!" roared Professor Federico Solco. "That's the way to describe that man's goings-on."

The professor was a fine old fellow who gave them the impression of moving within a picture-frame, but moving so gingerly that the onlooker tended to think, "Are my eyes deceiving me, or is that figure in the picture moving?" Back like a ramrod, fist planted on the table, clad entirely in black, his left trouser-leg permanently rolled up to the top of his sock, his right arm outstretched to test out and pierce the air with a silver-pommelled cane grasped by the ferrule, his moustache as white and wispy as the light of dawn, Professor Federico Solco was addressing the Executive Committee of the Panoramic Tower Company.

Buscaino, coat-collar up, head lowered, peering from beneath his eyebrows, was seated between Enzo De Mei and Leonardo Barini, the latter standing in for Rodolfo on account of the semi-literary nature of the person they were visiting. Tommasini was on his feet, in a pose from which Professor Solco, glancing at him from time to time, might possibly have deduced he was just straightening up after making a bow of assent performed while his eye was elsewhere.

"Delinquent, blackguardly, shameless, boorish!" repeated Professor Solco, while his breath, though not entirely disagreeable, was none the less a warning not to follow the speaker's own ideas and methods; at least if they wished to keep their hearts in good shape, not to mention their livers.

"I am an upright man, and despise this rabble of traffickers in science and art. Perpetual motion in a bottleful of gas! These scoundrels have made Natàca the laughing-stock of the world. And look at Morreale! A universal language based on tracing words to their roots . . . But what roots!! The Lord give me patience! Leonardo is derived from Leo (lion) plus nard (an aromatic balsam). My own name, Solco, is derived from 'solo co.', which means 'solitary company', i.e. a misanthrope, a hater of my own kind . . . Well, that's just because I've never thrown any money into the face of that contemptible worm . . . What's more, if individuals are doing badly, very badly indeed, is Europe doing any better? Who is there saying, 'For those I govern to seek happiness, moderation, prosperity and peace and quiet; I desire to bring them conditions under which may prosper the greatest blessings in life: art, the family, honest work and human dignity'? Ah, we must found in Europe the League of Happiness amongst those who (if you will pardon the expression) have no desire to be kicked in the bollocks and in return give firm assurance that they have no intention of so kicking anyone else . . . No, gentlemen, I am not joking . . . And you, dear colleague Buscaino, what is your thought on this matter?"

"My dear professor, I will not presume to use the term 'thought' for the seething that is going on in my head, when at my side I have you who are thinking, thinking properly, thinking admirably."

"Love, love, love! That is the root of the universe. Whenever the universe shows signs of drying up, look to the root of it, awaken it, revive it! It will become verdant again and once more emit its divine perfumes . . . But you do not understand me. You are too young."

"Professor," said Buscaino. "I fear you have just made a very serious statement."

"Why is that, dear colleague?"

"Because I understand you very well indeed, and this makes me think that I am no longer a chicken."

"Ah, you understand me, but not with the soul: you understand me with the mind. There, over there is the one who understands me entirely, the man who never speaks because he knows it is futile to speak a dead language, the language of the heart, the language of yore. There he is, the Friend!"

And so saying Professor Solco moved to the far end of the room to embrace a tiny old man sunk in an armchair, into which he had completely vanished except for two little eyes exceedingly quiet and still.

"This, this is the friend, the only person who understands me! With him it takes but the flutter of an eyelid for an infinite number of things to be said, comprehended and reciprocated. There is nothing in humanity which can possibly compare with this minuscule man whom you perhaps mistake for a person of small account, a mere nullity."

"Nullity!" exclaimed Tommasini, struck by an idea. "Nullity!"

"Keep quiet, Tommasini!" said Buscaino.

"At the demise of my unfortunately very very old friend, Signor Luigi Dilentini, to whom I now introduce you, my life will be over. I have charged him to say at once to the Creator, 'there is someone down below who wishes to wait not another minute! . . .' You want to reform the world . . . But what society, what form of cohabitation can supplant Friendship? Friendship, a Friend, heart, heart and heart again. And as for Jesus Christ, will we ever cease deceiving Him? How long will it be that while calling ourselves Christians and with one hand dangling the cross we wear round our necks, we think and say that it is better to kill our enemy than to forgive him, that it is prudence to distrust our neighbour, that we must jump on his neck as soon as he makes a suspicious gesture? True, infamy and iniquity are abroad in the world, but to regulate our lives as if we were surrounded with nothing but infamy and iniquity, to be forever on the lookout, to think ill of mankind, is a moral pessimism that embitters our young people, troubles our minds, squanders our substance, and deprives us of peace, of respite, of happiness. God in heaven, to live happily we have to be just a trifle ingenuous! 'Disenchantment will come!' you may say. It doesn't matter: disenchantment is a passing sorrow; but not to harbour any illusions about others is a perpetual misfortune, it is the end, the death of the soul. I never tire of repeating: love, love, love!"

"My dear professor," said Buscaino, having emitted a couple of brief coughs, "what you have just said is no small matter. No indeed, it is no small matter. It is, it is . . . it is what we expect of a discourse by Professor Federico Solco, our own dear, distinguished Professor Federico."

"Love, love, and love again!"

"Yes, love . . . Exactly what is recommended to the Americans by the famous Brellington."

"Brellington! But the man's a thief, a rogue, a scoundrel! He stole my ideas with the cunning of a child stealing figs from the priest's garden. His universal 'Society of the Dawn', on which every year they spend millions, and perhaps even billions, do you know where it came from? From here, every scrap of it!" And the professor crossed to the shelves and took down a green-covered file stained with coffee and olive oil. "It all came from here!"

"Ah, my dear professor," said Buscaino. "Thieves are a real scourge in the field of the sciences."

"No, don't say that! The field of the sciences is a highly noble one, inhabited by the cream of mankind . . ."

"Of course, of course . . . The cream of mankind . . . But just occasionally someone . . . I mean to say . . . That is . . ."

A brick – a somewhat large and heavy one – had stationed itself crosswise inside Leonardo's brain. The part of the brain to the left of the brick, and to some extent above it, was thinking, "The old chap's a good old buster." The part of his brain underneath the brick was thinking, "When will an enormous sneeze on the part of God or someone of lesser importance blow away this old man, and Tommasini, and the other old buffer, and Enzo De Mei and all these confused and pointless trifles like a swarm of gnats?"

As the reader can see, Leonardo did not imagine that the sneeze could blow away Francesco Buscaino. In fact, he credited this last with a certain solidity, as of a man who was alive and worthy to be alive. In a word, he had grown to admire him.

"Yes, my dear professor," said Buscaino, "I search in vain, in what you say, for a full stop, for a comma, with which to find fault. But alas, anyone seeking a defect in the discourses of our great Professor Federico is wasting his time . . . Love, love, love! That is the way of it. No doubt about it! I too occasionally think: am I doing good or bad by the respectable, unassuming city of Natàca, in presenting it with a tower a hundred and fifty feet high?"

"You are doing excellently!" declared the professor. "Excellently! You are raising this brutish rabble to a higher plane. Their insignificant gaze, launched from a height of a hundred and fifty feet, will learn to soar above base things. You are like the mother swallow who takes her fledglings in her beak and carries them to the treetop to teach them to open their wings. You are doing wonders . . . Furthermore, be yours a good idea or a bad one, the great thing is that it is a motivating motion, an idea which forces these men to get down to it and do some work!"

"Yes, dear professor," agreed Buscaino in a voice trembling with sincerity, "to get moving, to do something, it makes no difference how or where, but to do something concrete! Whatever one does is, in the last analysis, always well done; only what is left undone is done badly. To wake up in the morning and say to oneself: 'I have a purpose. The sun brings me a purpose.' To see a purpose in the sun, your own purpose that rises shining in the east and illuminates the world! To think, at sunset, 'There now, my purpose is going to rest, it is leaving the sky. The world is growing melancholy because my purpose isn't there any more. But no matter . . . In a few hours my purpose will appear again in the east.'"

These words, however confused and muddled, fell into place

in Leonardo's being like a paver's cobblestones into the spaces awaiting them.

"The heavy things of this world have to be thrust along by main force," continued Buscaino. "Machiavelli said, 'Allow me at least to roll a pebble.' They must be heaped up, used to start a pyramid that all can see from afar! To work, to get things done! . . ."

Every syllable of this was a cobblestone slotting into Leonardo's soft and yielding heart, taking its place beside the others in such a way that, when Buscaino finished speaking, where in Leonardo there had been emptiness, wavering, indecisiveness, the cobblestones were now hard packed. Yes, for a moment Leonardo's heart was capable of carrying the heaviest traffic of ideas and resolutions without showing the least crack. "O Buscaino, man of Providence!" he exclaimed to himself. "This tower you are going to build will give us a way of living properly, like men, for a year or two, and thereafter, under the safe wing of the money we shall have earned, to escape from here."

"I will buy your shares," said Professor Solco.

"Immediately?"

"Not immediately, but buy them I will. And lots, I may add."

"How many is lots?"

"I will buy lots, I say! . . . And now, dear colleague, leave me to my studies! Leave me to my faithful friend. When you arrived I was reading him the last chapter of a little book of mine. From what his gentle visage led me to understand, he approved. The only man able to judge me approves; he says yes, he says that my work is going well. Forgive me, gentlemen, but I can't help feeling happy about it . . . Goodbye, dear friends, goodbye."

Having made slight bows before the armchair in which glittered the eyes of Signor Luigi Dilentini, the four visitors took their leave of the professor. Putting his mouth close to the ear of their host, which from so close resembled a tiny picture of a shrub-covered island on which one might go hunting rabbits, Buscaino murmured, "Don't forget me, professor. You have no children, you are not married. Think of my tower as with the heart of a father. 'One who is not a father,' said Hegel, 'is not a man!'"

Professor Solco removed his ear from the vicinity of Buscaino's mouth. The latter cottoned on at once, and placed his own ear beside the mouth of the professor. "Dear colleague, I will tell you: my children are there." And with his eyes he indicated the booklets and manuscripts strewn on the table. "But those are all boys," he continued. "The tower will be my only girl-child."

"Well said, well said, professor! An excellent notion!"

And picking up his hat Buscaino hastened with all speed towards the staircase, where Tommasini was in the process of explaining something diabolical to Leonardo and Enzo De Mei. "That Signor Dilentini," he was saying, "is truly nullity itself."

"How do you mean?" asked Buscaino in alarm.

"He's nullity. He doesn't exist. What, for example, was substantially in that chair while he was sitting in it? Nothing! And now that we are gone, what is Professor Solco left with? With nothing, with nullity!"

Enzo De Mei threw an arm around Tommasini's neck, and being the taller of the two placed the other's bewhiskered head on the spot where folk-images of Jesus bear the flaming heart. "You're a clever dog," he laughed. "Nullity indeed! How d'you manage to think up such things?"

"Come on, let's be off," muttered Buscaino with a certain severity.

Down in the street he gave a glance at the second-floor windows, behind which Professor Solco was rereading his friend the last chapter of his book, a glance at Tommasini, who was pondering on nullity and nothingness, a glance at Enzo De Mei, who was watching Tommasini and knitting his brows in a painful effort of concentration, as if afraid that he might miss the other's least gesture; and finally a glance at Leonardo, who was smiling weakly; and having run his fingers through his hair both to right and to left, he scratched his head a bit.

VII

LEONARDO NO LONGER doubted that Buscaino had brought a little life to Natàca; he no longer had doubts about the utility of the panoramic tower, either spiritual or practical. It was not yet the light, it was not yet joy, lost four years ago and never since rediscovered; but it was an extremely workmanlike copy of them.

Rodolfo De Mei surpassed even Leonardo in admiration and loyalty to Buscaino. He had made up his mind to think well of Buscaino whatever happened, and not to permit himself any doubt or disappointment in his regard, however slight. And he got along splendidly. He had in fact realized that the human mind is really nasty if, once having agreed to think nothing but good of a person and, to be on the safe side, of the neighbours in general, the effort this mind puts into thinking is infinitely reduced, is reduced to practically nothing: a sign, therefore, that the human mind, when it thinks of a person or a neighbour without restraint, nine times out of ten thinks ill of him. But now, ah, what a relief! To think that one-tenth and to think like a gentleman, which is to say with kindliness and free from the carping spirit. Conscience (but is it really conscience? Yes, it seems to be: don't let's waste time splitting hairs!) approves with a radiant smile; one's health approves also. Rodolfo slept more soundly than before, and gradually began to put on a paunch of such becoming shape that it was plain to see it was of spiritual origin. Leonardo, giving it occasional little taps with his fingertips, could not help exclaiming, "You're happy, eh?", as if he had touched not a paunch at all, but no more nor less than moral contentment iself, in permanent, plumpish and yielding form.

Giovanni Luisi had gone through certain moments of mistrust with regard to the tower, but in time such moments became increasingly rare. In the sweet confusion in which he lived, in which everything appeared transformed into a state of shifting and changing vapours, one single feeling now dominated that agreeable chaos and illuminated it: the knowledge that he was an exceptional man, a man worthy of the important post which one day or another would be procured for him in Rome by his friend the general. At one time the tower scheme had been alternately brilliant and nonsensical, serious and pointless; now, Giovanni's inner confusion tended towards the bright side, and the tower scheme took advantage of this to present itself, with some degree of consistency, as a good idea. Yes, even Giovanni much admired Francesco Buscaino and thought of him as a man sent by Providence.

The one, however, who was dissatisfied with Francesco Buscaino was Francesco Buscaino himself. "In your notebook, my dear fellow," he told himself grumpily, "you wrote that by the end of June the tower would be built. June is past! So is the autumn. And we have not yet collected a single lira, let alone built the tower . . . Enough of these long, agonizing visits, which leave a little pinch of time on every insignificant object you see, on every word you have to say or listen to, like a sack with a hole in it that deposits a little pile of flour whenever you stop. Short visits from now on! Few words!"

Their visit to Duke Fausto Villadora had, in all truth, been extremely rapid, partly in deference to the wishes of their host who at a certain moment became aware that those four walls contained four pair strange lungs breathing, and viewed the air of the room as would a lambkin between the jaws of four lions. Furthermore, that fellow Enzo unhinged his jaw so, he could in a jiffy devour all the air in a cathedral.

"Yes," said the duke, in a tone in which he attempted decently to reconcile haste with glumness, "yes, you will receive my money. But there is no need for all you gentlemen to put yourselves out . . . Let Professor Buscaino come alone, and we will arrange the matter between us."

"Your Grace," replied Buscaino, "as soon as I receive your summons I shall hasten to you at once. What mechanical means, or what person, will bring me this summons? The telephone or the post? The coachman or the concierge?"

"We shall see, we shall see," said the duke, opening the door and leaping back behind the doorjamb, as if convinced that outside was a revolver-barrel waiting to get him. "My respects, gentlemen. My respects . . ."

His Grace had allowed many days to pass without sending any summons, and Francesco Buscaino was on tenterhooks. "I tell you," he declared to Rodolfo, while together they mounted and descended aristocratic staircases, penetrated into courtyards, peered at street-names and house-numbers, "I'd rather keep accounts for Al Capone than live here like a king! Christ alive! We don't even manage to distribute leaflets because no one here's prepared to take their hands out of their pockets for so little. After lunch the place is a ghost-town. Our menfolk collapse under the weight of their bellies and lie supine for three hours, waiting for the massive bulk under which they are lying to exhale its legs of pork, its wines, its farinaceous foods, and once more become light and portable. This, in Natàca, they call having a nap! Three hours, Christ alive, three hours of inertia, of the depths of night in the middle of the day, when right outside the sun is shining, the trains are running, and in every respectable place in the world people are thinking and working! And then, look how they walk! In the Corso yesterday I came up against a pretty dense little crowd. All those black overcoats, on the shoulders of which absent-minded hands placed now a palm, now a glove, now the tip of a lighted cigarette . . . And they moved, those pitch-black overcoats, no faster than the hands of a clock, and left not a chink between them! And I was in a hurry: within me I had the whole Niagara Falls, plus the Indianapolis races and the hurlyburly of Detroit!

I couldn't get by, my dear Rodolfo, I couldn't get by! And it's the same with everything else. I'm in a hurry, I have to build a tower, I have to join my little sweetheart in America. And in front of me are those black overcoats, scarcely moving and not a chink between them, not letting me pass, not letting me pass! And *still* I've managed to refrain from kicking them, Rodolfo. For three months I have been observing the silk stockings emerging below the ladies' skirt-hems and comparing them to the very finest embroideries from Japan; but I cannot catch a whiff of five lire, or even one – no, not so much as a red cent! For three months I've been buying booklets by Professor Federico Solco and asking the author to sign them, albeit in pencil. But he starts pulling out money and then pockets it again, giving me only a glimpse of it, as if those damned thousand-lire notes were printed only at one end and the rest was as white as snow. For two months I've been expecting Duke Fausto Villadora's doorman, but my hotel porter has not yet had the pleasure of passing the time of day with such an illustrious colleague . . . Then there's Tommasini who is trying to drive the *cavaliere* mad, and sending anonymous letters to the duke denouncing me as having arrived from ports where the plague is raging (and if I find him to be the sender of those letters, I promise you, Rodolfo, that no one on earth will save him from my straight right!). Then comes Leonardo, who's not willing to write a little piece mentioning our tower. He says that art should never stoop to such things . . . As if art weren't publicity and nothing but publicity! These poor sods should take a leaf out of the Americans' book! . . . And what about Giovanni Luisi who compares himself to Peer Gynt, no less! He, who sleeps twelve hours a day and reckons yawning more useful than breathing, compares himself to that man of action, to the conquerer of the world, to Peer Gynt! . . . And last but not least there's you, Rodolfo, who have not yet drawn a single line of your plan for the tower. Christ alive! It is lucky that in my own person I have a great ally: courage! Courage, dear Rodolfo, and will-power. And I don't intend to lose the game, not at thirty-nine! There, dear Rodolfo, on that sky in which the exhalations of your yawns most solidly condense, there, very shortly, I shall stamp my tower, symbol of activity, of alertness, of practicality, of wealth, of reality!"

Meanwhile Nello Tommasini was introducing Cavaliere De Filippi to a white-capped audience. In the great hall of the Rossini Hospital the convalescents from the operating theatres, delivered from their tumours and cancers, were listening to the *cavaliere*'s poems. They listened in silence, with wildly staring eyes, and that abrupt way of turning the head to the right, as when they were afraid of being abandoned by the relative come to look after them, that way of passing a hand across the forehead and opening their mouths from time to time to unstick the tongue from the palate. At the end they even managed to applaud. From then on, in the heart of the *cavaliere*, Tommasini occupied a truly enviable place. And the first to envy him was Buscaino, who found himself abruptly demoted from being the *cavaliere*'s dearest friend to being the friend of the *cavaliere*'s dearest friend.

That Tommasini was a fiend! He could work ten strings with two fingers. While he was gaining the affections of the *cavaliere*, and maybe sending anonymous letters to Duke Villadora, he made Signor Luigi Dilentini a popular figure in Natàca in the guise of "Nullity". When, well on in the evening, the old man left the apartment of Professor Solco, he used to go and sit in a second-rate café, the Prince Café, more commonly known as the Hooligans' Bar. He would sit in a small green-carpeted room which, through a glass-panelled door, was entirely within view of anyone standing at the counter. Tommasini, having drunk his coffee standing up, threw open the door, cast a glance into the room, saw Signor Dilentini sitting all alone and turned to his gang: "We can go in. There's no one here."

The party trooped in boisterously and sat down. Tommasini

pointed to the chair in which the old boy was sitting and: "Put it there!" he advised a friend uncertain where to lay his overcoat. "It's an empty chair."

Since the old fellow responded to all this by turning his head so slowly, so mildly, so wordlessly that the company wondered if he were not indeed nullity personified, Tommasini pushed the joke a stage further.

"Come over here," said he to a friend. "I want a private word with you."

And seating his friend on the old man's left, and himself taking the chair on the right, he started to talk as if there were no one in between them. The poor old chap got slowly to his feet and crossed the room, with stooping gait, his hat in his two hands and a smile which seemed to emerge from his baggy collar and feebly illuminate his scrawny neck and chin. He left the room.

"What's this draught in here?" yelled Tommasini to the waiter.

"Draught?" queried the other, taken aback.

"Yes, draught! The door's swinging open and shut like nobody's business!"

"But a gentleman just left . . ."

"A gentleman? I saw no one leave. And you," he turned to his friends, "what did you see?"

"Absolutely nil!" replied the whole gang.

This joke had by now entered the public domain, but naturally not everyone played it with the same finesse as Tommasini. Like a violin passing from hand to hand, not everyone performs well on it, and someone ends up by smashing it. At the cinema, for example, a certain swart, hefty youth observing that all the seats were taken and only one was free because there was nothing in it (or, rather, there was old Dilentini), decided to make a point of sitting in that seat. It took two *carabinieri* and much feminine censure to convince him that the seat was occupied.

"If you go on like this," shouted Buscaino at Tommasini,

"you'll be the ruin of me! If Professor Solco learns that you are the originator of this cruel joke, then we are lost, and justly so. Jesus, Jesus, Christ Almighty! . . . And I am unwilling to credit," (here Buscaino lowered his voice) "that it is you who, concealed in anonymity, are denouncing me to Duke Villadora as infected with contagious disease! Dear Tommasini, I am a man of honour, and I speak to you with open heart. I refuse to attribute these anonymous letters to you. But should the day come when the facts prove me wrong, that day I will remember that at the end of my arm I have a fist. You follow me?"

"Wild words, professor! You're right not to believe such an atrocity, but very wrong to admit that some day you might possibly believe it."

"The fact is that I am in your hands, Tommasini. And things are going from bad to worse."

"You are mistaken, professor. Things are going well. In a day or two I'll give you proof of it."

Tommasini's proof came swiftly. It was learnt from unimpeachable sources that Duke Villadora was willing to buy fifty thousand-lire shares, that in Cavaliere De Filippi's pocket was the money given him by his lady-wife, and that Professor Solco had been to the bank to change two money orders for large sums.

Buscaino was delighted. "Merciful God of the Atlantic and Pacific," he thought, "you are coming to my aid." To Rodolfo he bawled down the telephone, "I want the outline plan for the tower here tomorrow. Then I'll tell you the details. For the moment all you need to know is that things are GOING WELL! What's that you say? What's the matter with you?"

Rodolfo had nothing the matter with him. It was his brother, who every so often was seized with spasms of laughter such as had assailed him at De Filippi's during the poetry reading, and always on account of the thought that poor loonies were not mental deficients but jesters who at a certain point in their lives had sat back on their haunches like donkeys and refused to budge, had remained fixed, *fixated*. The previous night, too,

Enzo had woken up with the usual convulsion of laughter, and been forced to leave his bed and go barefoot into another room, like someone with a fit of coughing that will not let up.

"Don't give it a second thought," continued Buscaino. "Perk up and think, instead, that things are going well."

Rodolfo De Mei perked up and was happy. Along with him, Giovanni and Leonardo perked up and were happy. Life is fine, things are going well! When all of a sudden . . . But let us take things in order.

VIII

However much soldiers, nursemaids and children have for centuries studied swans on ponds, it has not yet been discovered what secret is concealed within those elegant and foolish creatures, those eyes like the eyes of staid young ladies, and that manner of gliding unruffled over the water. It must be a secret of great importance if, even in our own times, other soldiers, nursemaids and children feel the urge to devote many hours to the study of swans. And perhaps this study has entire millennia to look forward to.

Such were the thoughts of Tommasini as, with Cavaliere De Filippi, he paused behind a stockade of soldiers, nursemaids and children intent upon the swans on the pond. We are in the heart of the Public Gardens of Natàca. The pond is situated in a large open space from which radiate five tree-lined avenues, like spokes from the hub of a wheel. What their real names were we cannot say, but in common parlance they were distinguished as follows: the avenues of Famous Men, of the Loafers, of the Ugly Mugs, of Yawns and of the Dandies. It was from the Avenue of the Loafers that Nello Tommasini and Cavaliere De Filippi emerged into the open, the one reciting and the other listening to a number of poems, the birth-date of which would have been cause for envy even to the three-month-old baby snoozing in a pram a few yards from the pond.

"Do I make myself clear?" said De Filippi, attempting to shove Tommasini towards the Avenue of the Ugly Mugs, "do I?"

But Tommasini squeezed his arm and begged him to be quiet

for a moment: there before him was a nursemaid whose single visible eye so closely resembled that of one of the swans, and the latter was rushing her in such a manner, that it was pardonable to foresee some grand family reunion, and (who knows?) perhaps a slight scandal . . .

"Go on with you!" scolded the *cavaliere*, who suspected Tommasini of having queer ideas. "Let's get along."

"By all means, *Cavaliere*."

Having turned into the Avenue of the Ugly Mugs the *cavaliere* once again repeated the last six lines of his most recent sonnet, and clasping Tommasini ever more tightly to him he whispered, "You see what I mean, my friend? I do not believe that my books on the monogenesis of language are worth all that much. Nor do I nourish any illusions concerning my monograph on numismatics . . . But these little verselings, these trifling diversions, these thimblefuls of words in dialect, d'you see? Upon these, I believe, my reputation will rest!"

And since the verb "rest" is, in Natàcan dialect, pronounced "arrest", that rogue Tommasini, though full of regrets at pushing things so far and aware of the gravity of the consequences, could not refrain from murmuring, "They'll be arresting *you* one of these days, *Cavaliere*!"

And, wrenching himself free from the other's arm, he leapt away.

For a moment the *cavaliere* didn't twig; then, alerted by Tommasini's leap, and the scared, apprehensive expression with which the latter was peering at him through the leaves, he raised his stick and hurled it with all his might.

Tommasini, needless to say, skipped off without a scratch to show for it; but the events which should have led to the construction of the tower were gravely smitten. And the one who received the death-blow was Buscaino.

"He's ruined me!" he cried in one café after another. "That disloyal boy has ruined me. Thirty thousand lire, thirty thousand lire gambled away just like that, for a clever quip, while strolling along the Avenue of the Ugly Mugs! I knew that lad would be my downfall! Oh, but I'll shut his trap for ever! Upon my soul I'll shut his trap for ever!"

Unfortunately this episode seems to have given the signal for a long series of disagreeable events.

Signor Raveni had promised his son Lello that he would himself buy the shares in the Panoramic which Cavaliere De Filippi had rejected. But one morning Ingegnere Scannapini, waiting on the edge of a chair in the Raveni drawing-room, saw the door open half-way and Lello back slowly into the room, stark naked. The *ingegnere* cleared his throat, Lello turned and gave a yelp, the *ingegnere* gave another, and Signor Raveni arrived at the run. To tell the truth, the explanations which Lello gave to his father concerning this episode were not very felicitous. He was on his way to the bathroom, he said, when he heard footsteps in the passage and, supposing the drawing-room to be unoccupied, crept in to hide for a moment. But, his father justifiably asked, why go naked to the bathroom? And how can one hide in the drawing-room? And what if in the drawing-room, instead of the *ingegnere*, he had found the *ingegnere*'s delicately-nurtured wife? No, no, this was a sordid business, and probably that maid Luisa was at the bottom of it.

"Scoundrel! Imbecile! Excrescence! I'm not throwing you out because, for one thing, you must be mentally ill. But from now on not one of your friends will set foot in this house! And the very first one I'll kick in the pants, if he turns up here with that Rockefeller air of his, is your illustrious Professor Buscaino! Now get out of my sight!"

Buscaino had no time to tear his hair because he had to call with all possible speed on Duke Fausto Villadora, who wished to speak to him most urgently. Buscaino dragged Enzo De Mei along with him.

"Do come with me, my dear Enzo. Unbelievable things are happening! Signor Raveni . . . Lello naked . . . Naked, I tell you! . . . But you haven't heard. I'll tell you later. Let's get along to the duke now, and hope that at least this good gentleman does not go back on his word! I'll try to bring off that coup. I'll speak like an angel! I'll put my heart, my soul, my brains, my entrails and all the rest of me to work through my mouth. I myself will vanish, I'll be no longer there, I shall be but a mouth that speaks in the most tender and, if need be, heartrending manner . . . Duke, dear duke, do not abandon me! 'May my long study and great love avail me!' . . . (Dante, you know). But I'm burbling. And quite right that I should burble. If I lose the duke I'll have no one left but Professor Solco. You understand, Enzo? Only the old professor . . . But before that happens God will grant it me to shut Tommasini's trap for ever . . . Here we are at the door."

The duke, whom the two visitors found erect and immobile in the middle of a large chamber, bore little resemblance to the duke they knew, to whom their eyes had become accustomed. A dash of something new, and buoyant, and of extreme clarity, had entered into that nobleman's person and, while it had attenuated and apparently almost elongated him in the opaque, flesh-and-blood part of him, it had kindled strange flames in the eyes, the teeth, the fingernails. The duke seemed filled with a disquieting joy.

"Gentlemen," he said. "I have at last understood myself and my life. I am on the eve of becoming an unharrassed man."

"Your Grace," said Buscaino in the low voice of one who, alone in a church, is speaking to the statue of some saint, "Your Grace, this means that our highest hopes have been realized."

"I have got rid of the tiresome part of myself, and am about to put the other, the part that is weakest and most in need of assistance, under infallible protection. I have made a donation . . ."

"Donation?" queried Buscaino in a very different voice indeed. "What donation?"

"I have donated everything I possess to the Associated Hospitals."

"But this," cried Buscaino, "is, is, is . . ."

He broke off and, lowering his head, gazed at an ornamental tile on the floor, painted with eyes both large and small; and to them he confided all the despair he had in his own.

"Come," said the duke, "come with me."

Through a padded door the visitors entered a large room the windows of which, sealed by double slatted shutters and rimmed around with velvet, sent soothing splinters of light towards the ceiling.

"Those windows," explained the duke, in a voice ever more hushed, "filter the air. Here a man can breathe, even with his mouth open, without running any risks! The armchair which you see at the other end of the room is warmed or cooled by a device which regulates the temperature. Food will be delivered through this wall."

This said the duke pressed a button and in the wall appeared a yawning black cavity from which, like the tongue of someone blowing raspberries, there shot out a tray laden with dishes.

"I have books too! I have the telephone, I have the wireless! I shall be able to live here in blessèd peace."

"But this is a prison!" cried Buscaino.

"It is not a prison; it is a safe refuge . . . I am aware that human life ought to be conducted in the open air. But I am afraid of the open air. My mother, as she bore me, gave birth to this fear. I have made every effort, believe me, but I have never succeeded in overcoming it . . . But here I shall be at peace."

As he said this he appeared to be watching his own voice as it intermingled with those hangings, those velvets, those double shutters, and became hushed and lost in them. He watched them as a hunter watches his dog, as it goes ahead up the path that he too will have to tread. Yes, the duke also, with the passing of the years, will become wholly intermingled, and hushed, and lost in those velvets, those hangings, those double shutters.

"I shall be at peace . . ."

★

"Christ Almighty!" cried Buscaino as soon as he stepped outside the ducal abode. "You think you're embracing real people and your arms close on empty air: they slip away from you in the most ludicrous manner. Enzo, I need not to think about it for at least two days, or I shall go mad as well!"

Not to think, not to think about it! But to win! Buscaino's whole being took on the nature of a sharp pencil destined to write a single word: WIN. Away flew worries and upheavals, regrets and desires, and he was left alone with that fine black point which yearned to be able to write in full the only word it knew how to. Finally, Buscaino took four important personal decisions: to thrust aside, for the moment, any idea of going back to America; to desist from his diatribes against the Natàcans; to accentuate that lack of scruple which is the lubricating part of the conscience, the thing which makes the wheels of life turn most smoothly; to forgive Tommasini. The latter, on his part, had been at pains, in the course of a long letter, to show that Cavaliere De Filippi would not have provided the money in any case, for the simple reason that he did not have it and would never have wrested it from his wife.

"Yes, my dear Tommasini," Buscaino said to him one day pointing a lean forefinger at him, "I had made up my mind to shut your trap for ever. I left home with my pistol cocked . . . You have done me damage, very serious damage . . . But then I decided to bury all these episodes which in any case, on account of their woeful nature, deserve nothing better than a tombstone. But listen here, Tommasini: life is a very delicate matter with which I do not advise you to lark around too much. Life, my dear Tommasini, is labelled 'Fragile'. You imagine you can shove it about and knock it down with (pardon the expression) gross tomfoolery without breaking it. But on the contrary, it breaks. Look now at what has happened to Signor Dilentini! You called him 'Nullity'. You never said that he was sitting in a chair or walking along the street, but rather that he was *not* sitting in the chair and *not* walking along the street. And today death decided to join in the game, and Signor

Dilentini has indeed become a nullity. It will give you a jolt when I tell you that your joke was unconsciously perpetuated this morning by the undertaker lifting the coffin. Finding it so light, he said, 'But there's *nothing* in here!' I see you're upset. Let's change the subject. Let's talk about the tower. Of all my clients the only one left to me is Professor Solco; the poor professor much of whom will this evening be buried with his friend Dilentini! I am at my wits' end!"

"My dear professor," said Tommasini with all the depth of one matured by a sudden nasty shock, "my dear professor, had you but fewer scruples . . ."

"Me? Scruples? You are mistaken, Tommasini, quite mistaken. I have none at all. I travel without scruples, and am prepared to jettison morality like ballast if I realize the boat is sinking. The first law of morality is to live. The second is to win. The third is to obey the law of morality!"

"Well, if that's really the way things are, I'll give you a piece of sure-fire advice concerning Professor Solco."

"Do not hesitate to give it, Tommasini."

"Professor, do you know how to disguise yourself?"

"Aha, Tommasini, you ask that because you do not know my past life! The first chapter of my life, and the most important, has precisely that heading: 'Disguises'. I am famous in America for having transformed a number of young millionaires into women, dotards, cripples, hunchbacks . . ."

"But professor, would you know how to disguise yourself as . . ."

"Tommasini, Tommasini! Give me a wisp of hair, a scrap of cardboard and some glue, and I am no longer myself, but all mankind. The old maidservant handing me my hairbrush, my brother eyeing me from the depths of his armchair, my wife smiling at me in the mirror, the very dog sniffing at my shoes, can out of the blue meet a second self, come face to face with a perfect double. At four o'clock tomorrow Tommasini, if you so wish, you will meet another Tommasini and think you are dreaming. I am speaking in all seriousness."

"Excellent, professor! I'm delighted. I'll tell you my plan without delay. You must transform yourself into the spirit of Signor Dilentini."

"The spirit of Signor Dilentini! I don't follow you."

"What I mean is, into an even thinner and wearier Signor Dilentini who appears to Professor Solco while he is ascending the deserted, ill-lit staircase to his apartment, and tells him that it is imperative to buy shares in the Panoramic Tower."

"Look here, Tommasini, I'm not even going to talk over your plan. I accept it blindfold, I drink it in as the Russians drink vodka, chucking it into their bellies without letting it touch their palates . . . I'm off home at once."

And four days later Tommasini, much moved, witnessed the reappearance of poor Nullity. To tell the truth, it was a nullity with the addition of a certain quality which the Nullity did not have, a certain air of being an American in a hurry, a certain inner spur towards well-defined goals, a sense of being on the point of finding himself, fulfilling himself and, it might be thought, of bringing off a deal. In a word, a very fine scent might, within that nullity, have sniffed the odour of human flesh.

"Professor, you are perfect!" said Tommasini. "How on earth did you manage to muck up your neck like that?"

"Elementary, elementary . . . But tell me now, in all sincerity, who will Professor Solco see on the staircase tonight, his friend Dilentini or Francesco Buscaino?"

"Got up as you are, professor, to suspect you of being Francesco Buscaino would be like suspecting me of being Napoleon Bonaparte! This evening you will have the success you deserve. I've no doubt of it."

That evening, as Professor Solco with infinite weariness was mounting the first flight of his staircase, illuminated very wanly by light reflected from a far wall, he heard a sort of hissing and saw a shadowy corner come to life in a peculiar manner.

"Who's that?" he demanded. "Who's there?"

No one answered, but in the meantime the professor's eyes,

receiving rapid aid from his spectacles, perceived a spectral figure very much resembling his lost friend.

"No!" he cried. "No! It's not possible! I deny it, I deny it!"

The figure took a small step out of the corner, and the professor removed his right foot from one stair and placed it on the stair below, beside his left.

"No!" he cried again. "I deny it with all my heart and soul! I don't believe in ghosts, I deny that a living man can see a dead one! I deny it, I deny it flatly!"

And with a fearful shudder he raised his walking-stick, then lowered it again slowly as if it weighed a hundredweight.

"I'm not afraid, I'm not trembling, I am seeing nothing. I don't believe my eyes. It's all the fault of my state of health, and this damned darkness, and that scoundrel of a porter who doesn't keep a proper eye on the stairs."

"Federico!" intoned the figure. "Federico!"

"Even the voice, even the voice! . . . I reject the evidence of my aged eardrums! I denounce old age as a condition unworthy of a thinking man! I deny it!"

But at this point he lost his voice, and with it an inestimable ally. From the mouth which had uttered words so manly and encouraging Professor Solco now heard emerge an agonizing groan. The very company of his own body became insufferable to him.

"Federico, listen to your friend," said the figure, approaching with a sharp tapping of heels. But suddenly there occurred something diabolical: one part of Signor Dilentini, to wit the wig, came adrift and fell, and a face gleamed for a second while two hands flew to cover and defend it.

"Aah, you scoundrel, you ruffian, you bandit, you gangster!" cried the professor, jabbing with his stick at the flesh-and-blood man hiding his face. "You criminal, you madman, you villain, you gallows-bird!"

All this time the professor had his back pressed against the wall, as if he had unintentionally driven before him and cornered a cat and had no notion how to get it out of his path, for the more one shoos a cat away the more it feels threatened, arches its back and spits.

"Get out, you blackguard! Out from under my feet, you thieving scoundrel! Get out!" screamed the professor. But the stranger, still dangling shreds of the dead Dilentini, withdrew all the more into the shelter of the wall. His back to the opposite one, the professor sidled upwards, and for a moment these two bas-reliefs were mounting the stairs together, neck and neck. Then whatever was urging the stranger in a direction contrary to both their wishes suddenly snapped, and he rushed headlong down and the professor up; while on one step remained a grey wig, wherein glinted all the gentleness which formerly that staircase beheld, five or six times a day, on the head of a belovèd little old man.

At about two in the morning Professor Solco awoke. Things were not going well with him, for he had dreamt that in a bookshop window he had seen all his own books with their red and green covers, and everything on them was as it should be – publisher, title, year of publication – save for the name *Federico Solco*, which had been replaced by that of *Lewis Brellington*.

"Thief! Scoundrel! Blackguard!"

The professor switched on his bedside lamp and saw the portrait of his friend Dilentini spring into view on the wall to his left.

"I stood up for you!" he thought. "Dear friend, I defended you from the forgers of this city who thought they could copy you as if you were a bank note. Alas, for my reward the Creator has sent me nothing but a raging thirst."

And thinking thus he stretched out an arm towards the bedside table and with great effort raised the bottle to pour out a little water. But all of a sudden, amid the noise of breaking glass, he overbalanced. From the portrait on the wall his friend's glance could not reach him where he lay, but remained fixed upon the empty bed.

IX

NOT ONE OF THOSE seated in the avenue which the Public Gardens of Natàca had dedicated to Famous Men knew whose was the marble head which, from the top of a plinth behind his bench, watched him dozing. However, they all knew whose was that warm rosy ray that had settled on their shoes and was now showing signs of moving on, so that they were forced more and more to stretch their legs and stick their feet out. That ray belonged to the March sun; to the March sun which must at that time of day be at its zenith, but which no one glanced up at for fear of detaching chin from chest and dispersing the heat accumulated in the pleat thus formed. On the contrary (hat pulled down over the eyes, hands thrust into overcoat pockets, chin in the position we have described, legs outstretched and feet in the sunlight), anyone enticed by some noise above him to tilt back his head and take a look, was, on lowering it again and letting his gaze return to vacancy, left full of resentment against whatever had induced him to strain his eyes so far and so high. Others, on the sunny side of the avenue, sat with their legs straddled wide apart, their bootsoles turned inwards, revealing the holes in them, and their large hands dangling limply.

But the young men and the intellectuals disdained the benches and strode the avenues. Reitano moved at a snail's pace, his moustache completely covering his mouth like a dog's muzzle, halting from time to time to eye an ex-schoolmate (now a *cavaliere*) and wonder whether, in husky and intimate tones, he might not demand of him "Listen here, how many times a week do you go with a woman?" Sugarloaf Maled went about the gardens wearing his "King of England" look, not his "horsey" one, lest he should have to trot along the sandy row just inside the railings. Sugarloaf walked rather swiftly, tapping the treetrunks with his bamboo cane.

Avvocato De Marchi, his hands behind his back and his coat unbuttoned, like the twin doors of a loculus in which he had conserved his own august body, went to and fro with a rout of bandsmen and music-lovers amongst whom squabbles broke out as to the relative merits of Verdi and of Wagner; until he, turning slowly round to face the procession, delivered his own opinion and re-established peace. Among the group were Testaccio, whom the sun appeared to find too pale and clay-like to make any promises to shed its light on him next spring as well; Tommasini, who was staring at Enzo De Mei; and Enzo De Mei who was staring into space. Leopoldi walked by himself, tapping behind his back the thumb and index finger of his right hand against the thumb and index finger of his left, so that malignant tongues said that his hands, unbeknownst to their master and behind his back, had indeed – and this time genuinely – discovered perpetual motion. Also on his own went Professor Neri, a large notebook tucked under his arm, while the poet Nereggia, who was not fond of crowds because he was incapable of thinking about Sana Genoveffa without moving his lips and raising his forefinger in the air, and the poet Cavallero, who was incapable of thinking about Santa Rita without jerking his head this way and that like a horse dragging a cart uphill, left the Avenue of Famous Men, the one starting down the Avenue of Yawns, the other down that of the Ugly Mugs. They did, however, encounter each other from time to time and look daggers. The eyes of Nereggia, full of Santa Genoveffa, and those of Cavallero, full of Santa Rita, flashed like the windows of two rival shop-fronts.

Among those who had gone as far as the swan-pond (a very rare occurrence, since the young of Natàca had no habitual place to sit, but shunted up and down the Corso like a train which try as it might could not leave the rails) were Carlo Dalbi in a shiny green overcoat; Ninì Padeni, brisk, lively, always in a rush and never getting anywhere; plus Giovanni Luisi, Rodolfo De Mei and Leonardo Barini. The spring sunshine had also summoned to the pond the "Great Lizard" and his cousin the "Great Lizardess". Lello Raveni had hopes of meeting the maid Luisa in the wake of his parents, and crossed and recrossed the Gardens in every direction, like the tail of a snake in search of its own head. Every ten minutes on the dot he emerged into the open space round the swan-pond and stopped there for a moment to pluck at his moustache.

The sky was blue and shining, and the Mountain floated in its midst all white with snow.

"Yes," thought Leonardo, "it's really true. Since Buscaino has been amongst us things have done their utmost to smile, and can be likened to joy. Oh, I know very well that the smile isn't a real smile, nor the joy real joy. But it's better than nothing! This man, determined at all costs to give some substance to our lives, has my heartfelt gratitude. His efforts are magnanimous. And then tomorrow, when the tower is no longer a dream but a reality, when the Natàcans are heaved up to look at the panorama of the city (as if in fun, but the sort of fun that gradually becomes a serious business matter) and the modest lire of the citizens roll our way, and suddenly a decent sum of money in our wallets whispers to us 'You can go now! You can leave Natàca!', ah then! . . ."

Giovanni gave Leonardo a shake, and pointed out how lovely was everything in the garden, even a little mysterious maybe. "Take a good look," he said, and Leonardo took a good look.

Professor Luigini had halted beneath a tree whence descended a green light which seemed the ray of some noble sun, the noblest the sky could offer, and dedicated to him alone. An old man in a velvet overcoat was having his photograph taken at the foot of a statue, raising his face with such nobility that the statue looked like a quaint and foolish passer-by perched on top of the column, while he resembled a fine, austere statue placed unpretentiously upon the ground. Maria Careni emerged from one of the avenues and was swallowed up by the shadow of a pinetree, and whereas her whole figure was bedimmed, something about her began to glow with such fervour that Rodolfo wondered what was up with the girl. The face of the "Great Lizard" became as kindly as could be, as charming as could be, as straightforward as could be, and all the swans gazed upon it, some with the left eye, some with the right.

"There really *is* something mysterious about," thought Leonardo. "Natàca's different since Buscaino came. You feel that one person's will-power forces both people and things to accept the hard struggle to defend themselves or else give in."

"Will-power, will-power!" Buscaino was thinking, as he sat in a secluded part of the garden. "Where are you hiding? Is this the way to help me? Do you admit that the Natàcans can get the better of you? Is this how I've brought you up? Is it for this I took you to America? Is it for this I went hungry and homeless? Will-power, fallen angel, haven't I told you, repeated it time and again, that when you are alert and prompt and on your feet nothing can stand against you? Will-power, my will-power, take a tip from these stones beneath my feet, make yourself as they are, nay, a thousand times more so. Will-power, with your aid I shall if I please raise not only Natàca, but the sun! Will-power, you doze off easily in these southern climes. Ah, it's only now I realize that all these mornings I have got up and you have stayed abed. Like a slugabed bride you are slothful! . . . And while you sleep Cavaliere De Filippi slinks away, Duke Villadora is lost behind a padded door and Professor Solco dies! Will-power, I am forsaken!"

And so thinking, he got up from the seat and began walking jerkily up and down the little clearing until, turning into an avenue, he travelled the length of it at full speed, casting rapid glances at all those men sitting there yawning, those figures seemingly with the weight of iron and the consistency of rags, on whom Buscaino's will-power, crying "On your feet! Rise and shine! Follow me!" struck like the tails of certain comets which emerge from the depths of the universe and seem bound perforce to destroy the earth and carry it off; yet when they are near turn out to be more tenuous and insubstantial than the mist, and fly away silent beyond our planet, which has remained oblivious.

"Will-power, you are too weak to raise such leaden men! You are the soap bubble that presumes to lift a calf in the air. You must fortify yourself, grow a hundred times stronger. Come back with me to the hotel, and in two days I will train you to lift the world!"

At the end of the two days Buscaino's will-power launched itself from the hotel like a ship from the slips. It sought opportunities to put itself to work, it demanded concrete proposals.

Naturally, the one to make the proposals was Nello Tommasini. In his opinion they ought to address another section of the population of Natàca, one so far thoroughly neglected in business matters: the Maltese Hooligans.

All the young men in Natàca, even the characters of our story, belonged to a greater or lesser extent to the race of the Hooligans, but those to whom Tommasini alluded, the Maltese Hooligans, were so to speak the thoroughbreds, the direct, uncontaminated line of the race. These Hooligans were physically conspicuous for a certain coaly blackness; and coal appeared to be the main constituent of their bodies, showing up in their hair, which generally speaking stuck straight in the air to a great height and in a solid wedge, so that only very skilful hats were able to ride on it, and also in their eyes, their beards, and a myriad of tiny holes in the skin through which this coal appeared on their faces and all over their bodies. Spiritually they were more complex than one might think. Almost all of them were bachelors whose fathers were still living: fathers with whom they were much wont to quarrel, sometimes violently. (When they married, or lost their parents, their hooliganish nature underwent transformations so profound as to seem obliterated, save that it reappeared, in its purest form, in their sons.) They were dab hands at billiards; they dressed meticulously, with a preference for striped trousers, black jackets, red or lilac-coloured overcoats, green hats and patent-leather shoes. They attached little importance to a number of pretty serious matters: their view of human relations mainly took the form of elbowing, slapping people on the back and even tripping them up, though they were prepared to attribute unforeseen importance and seriousness to the fact that some gentleman or other had addressed them before being introduced, or had asked the time while they were in the company of a woman. In this last case the brawl that followed was anything but a joke, and everyone remembered it for years.

They loved to have themselves photographed; so much so that the shop-windows in the Corso were, all the year round, crammed with the heads of Hooligans. They went every Sunday to Mass. They believed very little in God, but a great deal in the palm-leaf they took home, blest by the priest, on Palm Sunday; they were constantly on the brink of marrying the boarding-house or Palais-de-Danse girls; at dead of night, howling at the tops of their voices, they would drive around in low-built but not really very fast sports cars; they were wealthy, and in their wallets (along with a lock of some woman's hair and snapshots of beach scenes of themselves stripped to the waist supporting a pyramid of friends) they always kept a nice wad of five-hundred and thousand-lire notes.

Buscaino wedded his own life to those of the Hooligans. Late night often found him in a cloud of smoke, bent over a billiard-table, his eyes fixed on the white ball as on a little world in which – more likely than in this one which has Natàca in it – sound projects perhaps obtain the necessary assistance. On the nape of his neck was a cone of light which never forgot to pick out the new white hair of the week . . .

On Sundays, wedged into a tiny car, of which they left the doors partly open in order to poke out whatever legs or elbows could find no room within, crushed between the beefy Hooligans, he sped about on the Mountain. He was present at the brawls that broke out at level crossings, involving the carters to whom a short while before, as he whizzed past their cart, the man at the wheel had shouted something in the nature of "You're half asleep up there, and all this time your wife is . . . !" He danced with girls in green shoes or gold shoes. He gave his opinion on the intention, evinced by his friends, of hiring out the furniture of the paternal abode without letting the old man know, or positively selling the family vault, in which no one was buried but their grandfather, and for which some fellow had offered fifty thousand lire without the bones and thirty thousand with.

In June he took part in the siege of the "Continental" schoolteachers sent by the Ministry to run the state examinations. During that period the Hooligans' cars were chock-full of petrol, their engines turning over noisily near the doors of the hotels or the meetings from which the President of the Commission would shortly emerge. Buscaino rendered inestimable assistance, succeeding in striking up a friendship with even the strictest of the examiners and with the president in person. As a matter of fact, they thought of him as a colleague. Excursions were made up the Mountain and along the coast; the Hooligans had smiles and to spare for those bearded men who had the goodness to let themselves be whirled along at fifty miles an hour. It looked as if everything was set fair; but on the last day of July, while propped against a glass on Buscaino's table stood a picture postcard signed by those same professors, with greetings from Milan "to you and your dear, hospitable friends", it was learnt that the "hospitable friends" had been mercilessly flunked by the authors of the postcard.

Leonardo, Giovanni and Rodolfo followed Buscaino's manoeuvres from a distance and much enjoyed the spectacle of such energy and spiritual enterprise. In the evenings, at Giovanni's, they talked about nothing but him, and it was as if a reflection of that activity touched their faces, they were so lively and animated.

Thus passed another year. A year of enormous efforts but no practical result whatever.

"You've tied one end of your string in my mouth," cried Buscaino, "and you've all been tugging at the other. Tug, tug, tug, and something has eventually popped out, though it isn't a tooth: it's three years of my life, a considerable portion of my existence!"

Smiling wanly, the three friends confided in him that their own lives had been bereft of six years, six years stuck in Natàca. "My dear Buscaino," said Leonardo, "Natàca never lets you go."

"No, Leonardo, I am a man of action! I came to transform Natàca, not to be transformed *by* Natàca. My wings are not yet limed. When I wish to I shall spread them and fly away!"

And one morning he had already put on his overcoat and his travelling gloves, and telephoned for a taxi . . . But a hand on his shoulder stayed him: the news of something sure-fire, absolutely sure-fire, caused him once more to stay on in Natàca.

X

THE HOOLIGANS, who were certainly not lacking in fantasy, had sometimes imagined that one of the more emancipated organs of the human body, the heart for example (though admittedly the heart was not the only organ taken into consideration), could succeed in living off its own bat, detaching itself from the breast in which it belonged and returning to it at intervals, like a sailor to his ship at moorings. The heart (say) perceives a beautiful girl about to enter a certain café and take a seat on a certain chair . . . Very quietly it slips down from the breast, slithers along the pavement, clambers into the chair and there remains, indistinguishable from the cushion. The girl comes and sits down and the heart now has her pressing on it, and on behalf of its master brings to pass the long-awaited moment when that girl would be pressed to his heart . . . At night, when the body is weary but the sentiments know no rest, the heart makes off over the rooftops, over the darkling town, towards those little red-tinged windows through which from time to time may be seen the shadow of a girl, toothbrush in hand. At dawn the master hears a scratching at the window, and filled with he knows not what sort of bliss he throws open the window and the heart, a little tired, perhaps, and a little frightened, like a cat that has been out miauling all night, backs up against the window-frame. Then, realizing that it has been forgiven, it leaps into the arms of its master and, puffing itself out, fur on end, allows him to stroke away the dew and the chill that have fallen upon it. Then it re-enters the breast and goes quietly off to sleep.

Man's fantasy is a fairly freakish thing, but it cannot be entirely lacking in reality, if something of the same sort was happening to Buscaino. His will-power, in that very period when he was struggling in vain to enlist the support of those of the Hooligans who were out on bail, unbeknownst to him had penetrated the District Prison of Natàca. There, by means of dogged exertions, it had converted and convinced certain other Hooligans who, lying prone on unyielding bunks, were still waiting to be sentenced for planning a *coup de main* against the Republic of San Marino.

These youths, who had not the least notion of where abouts in Italy the Republic of San Marino might be, and were lamented by their fathers as hapless innocents, mere children mistaken for thieves because they were playing at cops and robbers, wrote home to their families that they would endure imprisonment in a tranquil and even a happy frame of mind if on the north side of the city, just a short way from their cells, Professor Buscaino's tower were to rise. It was, in the opinion of all of them, a first-rate brainwave, and the pity of it was that it had not been afoot in Natàca when their own minds had been seeking a scheme to give them something to chew on – and at that time had found nothing better than the *coup de main* against the Republic of San Marino. They begged their mothers to purchase shares in the Panoramic Tower Company. They begged their fathers too, and their younger brothers, and their sweet patient sisters.

An entreaty, this, which came from that same darkness whence an empty plate returned on New Year's morning, accompanied by a note: "Mamma, that was such a super cake! All night long I wept and thought about you!" Such an entreaty did not go unheeded. At sunset on the very day when he was about to leave Natàca, Francesco Buscaino found himself with thirty thousand lire in his hands, the fruit of a first downpayment. Thirty thousand lire! Thirty thousand of the real stuff!

For some time he remained prey to a disorder somewhat

resembling the last wobbly spins of a top before it stops.

"Thirty thousand! Just like that, at the last moment! Cash, too . . . yes, hard cash!" But he soon recovered a grip on the reins of his being: "Well? What's so odd about that? Wasn't it obvious I was bound to win? How could it have happened otherwise? And after all, no great victory – a man like me against such people as the Natàcans!"

All the same, he did not succeed in preventing, either in his own heart or in those of his friends, the great outbursts of jubilation that make a man feel that his childhood is still within arm's reach.

In a single night Rodolfo made the drawings for the tower, and they were a mighty fine piece of work.

Leonardo heard tap-tapping up there at the tiny window through which, at one time, the light used to stream. That morning he almost believed that joy had returned: the song of a goldfinch seemed to him beautiful, limpid, full of promises, as it used to be in the old days of light. He leapt from his bed and went out to listen to that song. Yes, he recognized it; yes, it had all the sparkle of once upon a time. A short while later, it's true, the song was no longer the same, no longer held out any promises. But what of it? The faithful servant waits for the master absent on a long journey. Everyone tells him his master is dead. But none the less, the faithful servant waits. One night he hears the shuffling of feet in the hall. He leaps up, lantern in hand . . . No, it is not his master. But what matter? It is not him today, but tomorrow it will be. As for that shuffling of feet, the servant must have dreamt it, but it is a dream of good omen. This tower project, under way at last, was of a certainty a good omen.

Buscaino allowed the mood of exhilaration to find the expression that appealed to it most. Excursions up the Mountain, dinners in small restaurants along with crowds of Hooligans, singing, shouting . . . All of a sudden you are conscious someone is shoving a lump of ice down the back of your neck . . . Lello Raveni pulls out a revolver and lets fly at the glasses . . .

It's possible that the car might stop and five pairs of hands lift you up and dump you in the road in the middle of the country; whence, in the morning, you return to town on foot . . . It is also possible that someone might hold your nose and someone else tip so much wine into your open mouth that it stuns you on the instant like a blow. But, all things considered, this is hope, happiness, the gratified desire for a better life. And Buscaino let things be.

Less than a fortnight later the works for the foundations were already under way. The whole town turned out to watch the navvies sinking lower and lower into the hole from which they shovelled out the earth. Hands clasped behind their backs, Leopoldi and Nereggia watched the tiny workmen, as the depth increased, much as one might a body of pioneers setting off for the centre of the earth. The "Coronets Club" opened a new window on its north side so as to enable members to follow the work on the tower in comfort. The ancient Duke Robertoni, the first to look out of this window, on seeing Buscaino in the distance waved his arms about and shouted, "Greetings, greetings to the wealthiest citizen of tomorrow!"

Buscaino was much stirred as he looked at all the rock and stone and gravel cast up by the excavation, like one who after atrocious agonies regards the stone which the surgeon has that moment removed from his body, with benevolent reproof at first, but finally with the geniality of one who has forgiven.

"Sometimes in my hours of depression," he said, "I used to take long walks around these parts. On reaching the prison wall, with the tower on my mind as ever, I would stop and say to myself, 'True, I do nothing but think of the tower. But the poor souls shut up within these walls, who have arrived at this hour, the self-same hour shown on my watch, at the end of an interminable series of identical hours, hours of silence and solitude: what are those poor souls thinking of now?' Who knows what thoughts I imagined them having. But in fact those poor souls were thinking only of the tower. Like me!"

PART THREE

I

THIRTEEN YEARS had passed since Leonardo, Giovanni and Rodolfo had settled in Natàca, ten since Buscaino joined them, seven since the laying of the foundations for the tower. And if during these years the ringing of the masons' hammers hadn't chanted, "You are doing something, you are building this tower, you exist, you are living!", then you would truly think that God wants to pass off thirteen years as a single, uneventful day and make the burden of life a mug's game.

Work on the tower had been neither swift nor continuous: various contretemps had occurred to interrupt it. But to our friends its resumption was always like the recurrence of a pleasant, sonorous, friendly sound through the fog, reassuring us that the ship we are aboard is not veering out to sea, but coasting the mainland. It goes without saying that if in those thirteen years they had done nothing concrete and useful, the words "Forty years old! I'm forty years old!" which seemed so queer, sometimes meaningless, when they were alone at night in their bachelor beds and groping for the switch to turn off the light, would have become irksome and disagreeable. But such was not the case. Enough to go to the window and wipe off the condensed breath to see in the distance, over the black backs of the rooftops, the panoramic tower, its top terrace capped with a green cone and its stairway winding round its flanks. Far off in the dark of the empty sky, the sturdy tower! There it stood, solid and lofty. It spoke of hard work. When God on the day of judgement asked "What have you achieved?", it would slowly approach and answer for them: "They made *me*!"

Nevertheless, despite the tower and the eulogies it brought raining down upon Natàca, there was a something which complained and protested, a point in the air at a particular height above the ground (the exact height which the head of a boy born thirteen years before would now have reached), which said to Leonardo, to Giovanni, to Rodolfo: "You didn't father me! You didn't want me here! Why not?"

This point, this point in the air, was truly unbearable: it moved about, it followed them, it walked at their sides, it planted itself before them.

But the three friends had a remedy for this, also supplied by the providential Buscaino's panoramic tower. "Stop that, now!" they would inwardly bellow back. "You weren't born thirteen years ago so as not to be born poor. If you're born in a year's time, you'll be born rich! The tower is finished; we only need another month's work, plus official permission to open it to the public."

In the meantime they made and unmade thousands of plans. They calculated that after being in action for four months the tower would have earned enough to enable Buscaino and the three friends to quit Natàca.

Giovanni planned to take his departure by sea, Leonardo and Rodolfo by land routes. Leonardo meant to spend a month in Naples and one week in Rome. He was frightened of Rome, as a city which no sooner received him within its walls than it packed him off back to Natàca half-demented. Rodolfo hoped to go . . . He didn't quite know where, but he wanted to spend weeks and weeks on the train; he wanted to take his rest on those jumpy bunks after so many nights in his inert, impassive bed.

Giovanni, for his part, wanted to rove around the Mediterranean on board a little merchant steamer, lying about on coils of rope, chest bared to the sun and the wind: "We're young, aren't we?"

"Young?" queried Rodolfo. "At forty!"

Giovanni's face clouded: "Forty!" he exclaimed. He felt his chin, his forehead: still the same. Within him nothing had altered. How come he was forty? Twaddle, this being forty.

Just as the clouds made for the green pinnacle of the tower, but passed without bearing it off with them, so gloomy thoughts, though making for the topmost and most fragile part of a person, did not cause it to waver in the least.

After so many days – by now we should say years – of work and worry; after wresting stone after stone from slothful Natàca to build high the tower which now stood unsheathed in the sky, and oftentimes wore a look of encouragement, like that of one who has climbed higher than others and, seeing further than they can, reassures them that all is well; after overcoming the distrust, indolence and sneers of the Natàcans; now that they were about to celebrate victory in fact, it would have been wrong to fall prey to melancholy.

A month to go, a month to add the last few steps to the staircase . . . one little month!

The early days of that month were occupied with planning a banquet for a large number of guests, to take place in the grand reception room on the second floor of the tower. Invitations would go to all their friends and all the shareholders, as well as a great number of girls (girls? women who had been girls when they started thinking about the tower). Rodolfo had nothing further to design, now that every pencil-stroke he had made on those sheets of paper (which throughout that famous night had slid down to the foot of the bed) had deserted his studio, and were practically looking down their noses at him, from their proud position as stone, wrought-iron and cement; so he wrote, crossed out and wrote again the bill of fare for the meal. They all agreed on "dead man's bones", the pretty little biscuits which every evening, displayed in the lighted windows of the Prince Café, would halt the passers-by. They were brought to the table in dishes the size of cartwheels. They all agreed on roast kid which, despite the strictures of Masolino Ricasoli, remained an animal much beloved. Indigestible on occasions . . . but to feel in one's stomach those mild, kind eyes, or rather the flesh of which such eyes had been a part, was mysteriously consoling, and made amends, with its heart-warming bliss, for any sufferings, however acute, of the digestive juices. They also agreed that immediately after the dinner there would be a dance. With hop, skip and jump they'd shift the kid from their stomachs to their heels. Ah yes, there'd be a lot of laughs . . .

"Just what the doctor ordered, now that we've won," said Buscaino. "Plenty of laughs!"

"And plenty of departures!" added Rodolfo.

"Departure, later on, in our own good time. You are too wrought up, my friends."

But they were not the only ones. The whole of Natàca was in a turmoil. It was the first time that a dream of this kind, so personal, so Natàcan, and therefore so close to their hearts, had ever come true. The searching eyes that sallied forth at night from third and fourth-floor windows and wandered about the sky, on striking the soaring shaft of the tower, rushed back to their masters; like children exploring through the rooms of a house, who suddenly discover something that scares them by the way it chimes in with certain intimate desires and aspirations. Whereas in the morning the tower was the destination not of eyes merely, but of people in their entirety, standing round in a circle drinking in its broad base (for it tapered towards the top).

"This tower is just three boxes one on top of the other," observed someone.

"In my opinion," pronounced another, "the only thing wrong is that the stairs are stuck on outside, *and* too narrow."

"If you ask me," said a third, "it would have been better to put the reception room on the first floor, not the second."

"What price the pinnacle?" asked a fourth. "Why have such

a thing covering the top terrace? All it does is block out the sky."

But the majority were enthusiastic: lovely tower, sturdy tower, excellent tower, indispensable tower, charming tower, stylish tower.

Leonardo, Giovanni and Rodolfo received compliments at every step they took. In their homes the telephones never stopped ringing, filling the little half-darkened rooms with huge words of eulogy, some of them spoken so loudly that they had to remove the receiver from their ears, and finally to toss it onto an armchair where it continued to bounce about at the mercy of those thundering tones – or sometimes pure and simple coughing fits, those of Avvocato De Marchi, in whose breast the music had been transmogrified all into hoarseness; nor was there discourse which he was capable, we will not say of carrying to completion, but of taking further than the second word, before it was lost in painful and noisy expectoration.

Lisa Careni, now thirty-one, also made her voice heard at Leonardo's; and it was still a young voice, still with a ring to it, a voice which for years held back a joyous laugh which had never found a chance to get into action, to make itself heard.

The old question "When is it you're off to Rome?", put to sleep quite some years ago, now returned to knock at the ears of the three friends, who replied with the high spirits of invalids on the way to complete recovery: "Soon, soon! And this time for real!"

"You too, Giovanni?" asked Lisa Careni.

"Of course."

"And what will you go to do?"

"That's a good one! To live, to live in Rome."

"Got a job?"

"No, I haven't. But what's that matter?"

The general had not kept his word; Giovanni had not managed to obtain a salaried situation. Job or no job, there was nothing more to be hoped for from the general, since the problem of his own situation now hung over him, and in a rather grave manner. For, he having died after rendering signal services to his country, it was as yet uncertain whether he should not be disinterred and translated to a place far more stately than is a common cemetery.

Buscaino, as usual, brought to all this commotion a sense of reality and a practical aim.

"We must buck up," he said. "We are almost through the tunnel. Soon we shall emerge to see the stars again. I have run out of patience, my friends. Ten years are ten years! The work must suffer no more delays!"

But the series of hitches was not yet at an end. One afternoon (amongst other things) Lello Raveni, who in those last stages had become an indispensable element, fell victim to a tragic mishap. His father had at last given his consent for him to marry the maid Luisa; and Lello was in bliss. Luisa, for her part, was happy in a rather alarming fashion; for when, in a home where she had washed the dishes, she found herself in the position of *fiancée*, she was seized with anxiety and practically with dread. In her bed as a housemaid she had slept so soundly that not even the shrillest of alarm clocks would wake her; in that of a bride to be she was unable to snatch a wink. She lost weight, becoming increasingly more refined and attractive, as if the flesh she was shedding was that which pertained to the peasant in her. Distinction began to transpire from every pore of her diminished body, like light through a window-pane polished over and over again. But one day, at Brighella, during a halt in a motoring trip, what do you think happened? Lello had got out in search of a farm manager to whom he had orders to give, and Luisa, seeing a church-door ajar only a few steps away, asked Lello's mother for five minutes' leave of absence and, crossing herself quickly two or three times, entered the house of the Lord. Fifteen minutes passed, then half an hour. Lello returned, but still no Luisa.

"What on earth is she doing all this time?" asked Lello irritably.

"Leave her be," replied his mother. "She'll be a while yet, if she's going to thank the Madonna for all her good luck!"

Finally losing patience, Lello went in – and you should have heard his howl! Slumped at a *prie-dieu*, Luisa had reclined her head on it for ever before the altar of the Madonna, a duster in one hand and on her face an expression so humble that she might have been asking the Queen of Heaven to take her on as a housemaid. Lello had fainted away. Now wrapped in a blanket and inert on his bed, he intended to stay there for years. His father paced up and paced down, seeking now one mirror and now another in which to hurl insults at his own face, calling it idiot! lunatic! monster!, because he ought to have realized that the poor girl was at death's door.

Lello Raveni will no longer speed off in his sports car, not to this town to order tiles for the tower's top floor, nor to that one to nudge a high official into getting an instant permit for its opening to the public.

Hitches were nothing new to Buscaino, but at this point his moral stamina reminded him all too poignantly of an undervest too often scrubbed . . . and scrubbed too often in unsavoury waters. There was also his "wee debt" at the hotel, which only his shameless relish for pet names could continue to so call. Certainly the first moral law is to live. The second is to win. And only the third is . . . to obey the law of morality . . . But debts challenged the conscience in a manner far from abstract and subjective; to wit, by means of faces so glum and pressing that if the highest moral law really is to live, then in order to obey it one must first obey the least of them, and obey the moral law. In other words, pay one's debts!

Buscaino had from the beginning scraped along by borrowing from people outside the hotel in order to pay his hotel bills, which amounted to keeping the faces of his creditors as far as possible from his own roof. But in the course of time the debts contracted outside to pay the hotel were joined by debts contracted inside the hotel to pay off the outside debts, until finally everything was in such a tangle that Buscaino had contracted debts both inside and outside the hotel not to pay off any creditor whatever, but simply to purchase on the never-never a few objects indispensable to the life of a civilized man; and thereby incur further debts. All this, however, would have been of scant importance if the wheel of wealth, which in his mind's eye he saw hoisted to the topmost point of the tower, had been able to begin its gyrations. Time was pressing. Nor did Buscaino quite have his old flair when it came to urging the shareholders to pay the last instalment, the one which would make it possible to complete the tower and write *finis* to this long-drawn-out overture. The shareholders replied that they had never failed to honour their commitments, and that they scarcely intended to turn miserly at the last moment.

"I know, I know, gentlemen," returned Buscaino, "but this is the country of hitches and delays."

"What hitch could there possibly be?" asked one old man, coughing into his closed fist. "There's no room left for them."

"Quite so," agreed Buscaino. "No more room for them."

All the same, a last hitch there was, and – the devil alone knows how – it suddenly found room enough to plant itself in front of Buscaino.

II

Vincenzo Bellini, as all the world knows, was born in Natàca. The music which this son of a city of swarthy men and black stones has left upon the air shines as white as May sunshine. "This is life," he cries, and throws upon the table a refulgent treasure. "So it is for me, and so it must be for everyone."

And God, on the other side of the table, drops his expression of irritation and abstains from saying what was on the tip of his tongue: "My dear boy, life is a far more chaotic and complicated thing. Don't embroil yourself in such matters." Instead he murmurs, he too in love with that young man, so proud, so candid, "Very well then. Have it your own way!"

Single-minded like all those who, by virtue of an early death, have not the future burden of old age to bear, he celebrates nothing but joy, the joy of loving, the joy of dying young, the joy of suffering, the joy of going mad, joy pure and simple.

His melodies, seeing that it was the centenary* of his birth, were echoing throughout the world. No orchestra on either side of the Atlantic but was full of that ringing voice. The wirelesses of Natàca, fishing in the evening betwixt America and China, landed nothing but the music of Bellini. Sets in the home relayed it on to the floors above and below, while those in the shops, loudspeakers at the windows, sent it forth to rain upon the passers-by. The latter stood shoulder to shoulder for hours at a time in the half-dark sidestreets, like flocks

---

* What careless fellows writers are! Brancati has confused the date of Bellini's birth (1801) with that of his death (1835). [Translator]

unexpectedly overtaken by nightfall and driven by the shepherd into the first courtyard to hand. Here someone has nodded off with his chin on a friend's shoulder; there a maidservant covers a glass of medicine with a corner of her shawl, leaving her mistress perishing of the toothache in some distant part of town.

But not only the wirelesses transmitted the music of Bellini. In the smaller alleyways the gramophones also poured out that music upon soldiers, frying foods and fish with staring eyes, and in the avenues sonorous notes, do, re, mi, informed the young lover that his girl was at the piano performing the very same.

In Natàca's great opera house the works of Bellini were in rehearsal. The following day all those who had been present, wherever they were and whatever they happened at that moment to have in hand or in mind, re-echoed the melodies heard the previous evening. As a man in a freezing climate goes enveloped in a cloud of his own breath, so every inhabitant of Natàca now went enveloped in the notes of Bellini. There was not a soul who, from near to, failed to manifest a murmur of melodies, a low whispering, perhaps the mysterious sound of his very own being. Anyone with a good ear, hurrying past a complete stranger and catching a wrong note on his lips, would stop and politely correct it; then continue on his way, bearing on his own lips the melody the other had been humming.

Born and grown old in Natàca, the music-masters who had spent their lives composing aria after aria in the hope of emulating Bellini, and every time asking themselves "Is this motif worthy of *him*?" now felt that all those tunes were not only worthy of *him* but belonged in large measure to *him*. However, the music of that man was so magnanimous and maternal that the tunes of the poor music-masters were not expropriated or swallowed up by it, but on the contrary were cleansed and supported, like the kittens a mother cat washes and lifts to their feet with her tongue. The music-masters of

Natàca, once over the first moment of uncertainty, decided that their works were not just beautiful and original, but beautiful and original to the highest degree.

But all this joy, this pure melody, went in at the ears of the Natàcans and came out through their mouths, but left their hearts in the murkiest of darkness. The faces humming those bold airs addressed to the moon, to the flowers, stolidly retained their accustomed gloom, like those grave, stone faces from which – without managing either to incommode or to amuse them in the least – there spouts the sweet laughter of water. All that celebrative sound, all that triumph of trills, made no change in the life of Natàca. At sunset, through the window-panes, the faces and figures of seated women little by little were lost as at the bottom of a dark pool; few words did the mother address to her daughter, and the daughter answered almost none; a gardener looking down from a terrace saw his donkey wrest his muzzle from the straw, and murmured "What's up with you, me darlin' heart?"; rocking an empty cradle, the pregnant girl thought with horror that before a hundred years had passed the tiny fellow now growing in her womb, even he, would belong to the realms of death; the populace was still determined not to take its hands out of its pockets or stay too long on its feet; Bellini himself, in the Natàcans' commemorative marble statue, had been unable to manage without sitting down, and from this commodious posture he darted at the clouds such looks as the members of the "Coronets Club", from their wicker chairs, shot at the girls as they hurried by. Nor was the piazza in which he sat a cheerful one, or even sufficiently well lit. The evening on which fell the centenary of his birth, at the very moment of the day when he emitted his first wail, and now in all the theatres in the world there were audiences on their feet with shining eyes, amid lights, orchestras, flowers: at that very moment, in Natàca, Vincenzo Bellini, looming white in the dimness of the piazza, heard only the cab-drivers arguing in loud voices under the palm trees, and saw but one poor woman, known as the Night Bird, who that evening had started her foray earlier than usual, sidle across the piazza limping a little.

He was much loved in Natàca, but by melancholy people in a melancholy way. Perched on a ladder the following day, the workman responsible for keeping him dusted gave him an indulgent smile and a gentle rub-down, as to a child who has been out in the cold.

"My fate is like Vincenzo Bellini's," thought Buscaino, his elbows on the sill of his window which by this time was among those poised in the dusky blue of the sky, high above the light shed in the streets. "I too am popular in Natàca, and I too in a melancholy way. I too have showered upon these poor townspeople something resembling *his* music, something gay and stimulating, a delight with a hidden goad to it, a motivating idea. But this ill-starred idea of mine, like a horse harnessed to a cart too heavy for it, has had to strain every muscle with the effort, strike sparks from the cobblestones, wear itself to the bone, and to take one step ahead has had first to attempt a thousand. That's why it's taken ten years to build this tower."

Buscaino lowered his brow onto his open palm and, prompted by the notes of a pianoforte rising through a rooftop as serene and straight as smoke from a chimney, continued with his thoughts: "Ten years! After so long a lapse of time I have the right – indeed the duty – to introduce the Buscaino of today to the intrepid Buscaino who once alighted at Natàca, and to ask them, 'Well, do you recognize one another?'"

But Bellini's music would not allow of his taking this view of life; besides, Buscaino was one of those who have always grasped life by the hilt.

"Let us not forget, however, the tower is built, the tower is standing! This loveliest of flowers which sprang, we might say, not from my head but from my heart, as I slept one midsummer night under the stars; this wondrous flower is *there*, robust and durable, loftier than the church-towers, close to the clouds! And before long, the exquisite perfume it gives forth will be neither jasmine nor lily of the valley, but wealth and prosperity;

and from this perfume, as a bee draws nectar from the flower, I shall draw the choicest of honey; and I shall store it in many little heaps, according to value, for my honey will be silver and my hives will be a mint!"

Thus spake the music to Buscaino. But in a while he straightened up, suddenly wary. The fact was that in Natàca you had to be wary of everyone and everything; even of this music which at first hearing had seemed an ally, but then of its own brought a setback and a delay.

On account of the Anniversary, in fact, the shareholders of the Panoramic Tower Company, who had had to subscribe large sums to enable Bellini to receive the honours due to him, had asked Buscaino to defer their payment of the last instalment. Then came a further blow: the official appointed to collect the promised Bellini subscriptions thought himself subjected to undue pressure, and addressed himself in such terms as "You can take time off, lad; there's no hurry for a job like that." Meanwhile a spurious official, brisk, polished, handsome, obliging, presented himself at the front doors of Natàca and snapped up all the sums destined for the festivities in honour of Bellini. It was not known to what actual festivities these sums were thereafter devoted. Some spoke of women, others of travel, but even with regard to the latter there was no agreement – some spoke of trains, others of steamers, others again of airliners. What followed without *any* doubt at all was a second collection of cash which naturally pushed the last instalment in favour of the Panoramic Tower still further into the future.

"My dear Enzo," said Buscaino, "you are at the moment the only sufferable speck in the whole of humanity, the only one without envenomed prickles, and on whom I can safely lay my hand."

Enzo was staring straight ahead of him, with a slight smile; but it was easy enough to see that this was not his number-one smile. The latter was still dedicated to the thought that poor loonies are jesters who at a certain point in their lives have refused to budge and have remained fixed, *fixated*.

It was a moonlit night such as had not been seen in Natàca for quite some time. On these nights the walls of the buildings, the asphalt of the roads, the whole scene is endowed with a grace which induces respect and reticence. The universe seems destined to beings far more de luxe than men; men who move, slowly, like muddy worms in a silver dish. Buscaino joined the tip of thumb and forefinger and flicked at his overcoat collar. But what renders us unworthy of such a shining, harmonious universe is not the ash on our suits, the crumpled collars of our shirts, our dusty shoes. It is the very fact of being men that strikes us as a little unclean. The other fact, moreover, the fact of having to die, accompanies us like a vile stench, forcing us to blush at every step.

"Yes, friend Enzo, this last month of work is bound to become a year! All it needed was Bellini, who was in such haste to be born that a century later he throws a spanner into the works of poor Buscaino. But poor Buscaino is not going to lose patience. He knows that life is a battle of patience: my patience against that of Natàca, the patience of art against that of matter. Life is Tom pestering Dick and Dick pestering Harry; or else, if you prefer, it is like that game you play as children, or with your girl-friend, when the loser is the first to tire of gazing into the other's eyes. We mustn't tire, Enzo, we mustn't capitulate! If need be we shall wait another year. The tower, which is this evening conversing with all the lofty and beautiful things of the sky, counsels its creators to wait with calm of mind. You, friend Enzo, will be my chosen companion in this last, brief time of waiting."

Enzo puckered up his face, as he always did when his number-one laugh, the one given over to his thoughts about loonies, began to rasp in his throat. It was plain that he was attempting to resist it. But all of a sudden his mouth, which he had clamped shut, appeared to burst, and the laughter blasted forth with diabolic din. With one hand Enzo covered his face, with the other he supported his belly under the blows hammering down from his lungs.

"Enzo, my dear friend," exclaimed Buscaino, "you can't go on like this."

But the young man was swaying this way and that on his heels, his body one great rumble, his eyes as if casting about for somewhere to throw something.

"Enzo!" shouted Buscaino, shaking him by the arm. "For God's sake stop it!"

Stop it, indeed! The laughter redoubled in vigour and volume, and having caused the young man to turn almost a full circle impelled him towards a house-front and obliged him to sit down on the steps.

Once seated, Enzo remained for a moment engrossed in silence. But then another explosion of laughter all but shattered his frame, and further gusts, each mightier than the last, forced down his head between his knees until it almost touched his feet. At each gust he grabbed hold of his ankles and heaved them towards him.

"Good God!" muttered Buscaino anxiously. "Enzo, enough of that!"

Enzo now gave every sign of having to throw up, to rid his very being of some blockage, and that his bellowing would not cease until he had expelled it, as you cough to get rid of a grape pip gone down the wrong way.

"My God, my God," murmured Buscaino.

A shriek of laughter, all but agonizing, suddenly told him that something extremely serious had occurred.

It left Enzo absolutely quiet, worn out. He even looked thinner. The ghost of a smile still played about his lips, and in his eyes, instead of expression, there quivered an apathetic yellowish light.

Buscaino took a step backwards, as it was brought home to him that the impediment Enzo had rid himself of with those blasts of laughter was no more and no less than his wits.

"Ghastly!" began Buscaino. "It's ghastly! . . ."

But then he saw it all as a dirty trick played by God on him, Buscaino in person. "You're trying to scare me!" he shouted, partly to himself and partly out loud. "You're trying to put my courage to the test. Well let me tell you, whatever form Your will is disguised in, even this, a friend going mad on me in an empty street, I shall recognize it; I shall divine, even beneath such suits of woe, that You abide, and that all things considered You love me."

For a moment the thought of himself vis-à-vis God was so strong that in the blow that had struck him like a bolt from the blue he could see nothing but a joke, albeit in pretty bad taste, played on him by destiny, a "Boo to you!" shouted at him unexpectedly from behind the wings of appearances, on an evening when the stage, because of the full moon, was the acme of tranquillity and splendour.

But then the young fellow sitting there on a step, with his black-shod feet near a pool of moonlight, his mouth falling slackly open and emitting over and over, like a pathetic dribble, the word fixated, fixated, fixated . . . that young fellow who was someone's son, someone's brother, and only a moment ago was so winning in his affections, began to recall Buscaino to thoughts less selfish and abstract, thoughts more humane.

Buscaino took him by one arm. Oh, there must be something winged in a man's wits, for this lad here is as heavy as a great boulder!

"Come on friend, up we get!" said he.

At first Enzo showed no sign of understanding, then he suddenly stood up and went along with Buscaino, who led him by the arm. Slouching, black, ungainly, he never ceased babbling "fixated, fixated, fixated . . ."

When he thought that he had come to that part of town with a dear and rational friend, and was returning with a madman; when he looked at the moonlit scene and saw himself, as tiny as could be, laboriously hauling along that bulky creature who was no longer a part of the human race, Buscaino felt his heart seized as if by pincers and crushed to bursting point.

"I won't think about it," he decided angrily. "I won't think about it any more! Life must go on . . . It can't stop here . . ."

And giving a squeeze to the hefty arm in his grasp, he quickened his pace.

The resolve not to dwell upon what had happened, to lock up his heart, to be tough – a resolve in which frail spirits find justification for not suffering unduly – was, after several hours of desperation, adopted also by Rodolfo.

And one evening when, launched by loudspeakers, the voices of the dead, the voices of famous tenors and sopranos of former days, were in flight in the skies of Natàca, Enzo departed, accompanied by a doctor, to a mental home. On the station platform were Rodolfo, Buscaino, Leonardo and Giovanni. Enzo, shoved forward by the doctor, appeared at the window of the moving train, but his gaze fell not on his friends, not even on his brother, but on a black cat waiting for the train to leave in order to cross the rails.

"There, at least, goes someone who's managed to leave Natàca," said Giovanni, waving a green silk handkerchief with ever diminishing vigour.

That evening Rodolfo brought Lisa Careni the present of a wooden puppet. In one of the piazzas along the way he had passed a puppet-show with a big crowd clustered around it, and he too had stopped to watch. A boy lost in a wood meets a black-clad monk who offers to act as guide. "Mind now!" says the boy, seized by a sudden suspicion. "No nasty thoughts! As a He I left home and as a He I intend to return there!" When the show was over Rodolfo persuaded the puppeteer to sell him the wooden doll.

"Mind now!" said Rodolfo, working the strings. "As a He I left home and as a He I intend to return there!"

But he suddenly burst into tears.

III

THE DECEMBER RAINS; the midnight pistol-shots at doors and walls to scare off the evil eye on New Year's Eve; Santa Genoveffa's Day, with the black clad townsmen in white cowls; springtime with the first scorching rays of the sun and the shutting of shutters; summer, autumn, winter again . . . The everlasting passing of the seasons that drags along the living and the dead. But the new living closely resembled the dead; if old Neri's short overcoat waited in vain for someone to take it over, the idea of Morreale had found a new gaffer to do the rounds with it and defend it; and if Wire-Whiskered Willie had relinquished the free air for that of the gaolhouse, this time for life, prickly-pears still found someone who could, with threats, cram them by the dozen into some luckless mouth with not a gap to breathe through; and as many of those whose beat ten years ago had been the Corso were now beaten by the rain among dark cypresses, the footsteps which dragged over the lava flagstones were no less numerous or less leisurely than then. And the wind which came from Africa still never failed to elicit that prolonged creaking from the shutters and to counsel sleep; and the morning sky, normally of a porcelain opacity, tired the eyes and put them on the road to closing; and mothers, as they sang a lullaby to send their tots to sleep, raised their voices as if it were only Christian to project anything conducive to sleep as far as possible and reach the greatest possible number of ears. Stretched on their bumpy, lumbering carts, the carters, wherever they passed and at whatever hour, left all hearts closed and bowed down by their songs, like flowers by the frost at night. So the question arose: what purpose have so many sorrows, so many dead, if the new living with uncanny exactitude reduplicate the late lamented, and the new youth like the youth of yore does not know what to do in the evening, and the sound of the seasons is like the sound of water on the shore, and in the end is always the same; and maybe the sea, in spite of the glitter and roar of it, moves not at all? This anniversary year was wending its way like the rest of them, with the gait of an ancient and somnolent donkey. Unavailing were the thumpings on the rump it took from Bellini's music on the one hand and Buscaino's impatience on the other: it didn't even feel them.

One February day Buscaino, walking along a country road with some friends and seeing to right and to left the groves of lemon trees hung with golden fruits, so let his imagination run riot as to exclaim: "These are not fruits at all, but the faces of children hanging on the boughs. Small wonder if the new race of Natàcans is here about to be born, with green eyes and skins of gold: happy beings who will appreciate the work of Buscaino and see the Panoramic Tower as the first sign of the new annals of Natàca!"

But while waiting for these happy beings to descend from the trees Buscaino spent his days with men of the old stamp, those whose faces (as he put it) still bore signs of the darkness of the womb in which they were conceived.

"Oh dark, dark, dark!" he would say over and over on the long afternoons when there was nothing to do. "The good wives of Natàca ought to let a little light into their wombs, to open shall we say a window, and when they are on the verge of motherhood to swallow a sunbeam every morning."

In the evenings he too frequented Giovanni's dining-room, where the conversation still ran on marriage, on how Natàca wouldn't let one leave, on the light which Leonardo's heart had never seen again. And from Toulouse and from Budapest the wireless transmitted tangos, the chinking of coffee-cups and the laughter of girls.

Exuberant still was the bosom of the woman in the middle of the ceiling, whose rotundities hovered above the table, upon which (said Buscaino), if they were to fall, they would most likely share the destiny of doughnuts. Ruddy and plump as ever was Giovanni's uncle, Roberto Luisi; and discreet was the yawn which he yawned, this evening as every other, after hearing an hour of the friends' conversation and now on the point of rising with the same old phrase, "Lads, I have to work tomorrow. I bid you good-night."

What a town Natàca was: a mortar in which one pounded life without ceasing, but with no more effect than if it were water! Now that the masons' hammers on the tower were stilled, and with them that comforting voice saying "You exist, you are alive, you are doing something!" in the sudden silence, as when a train comes to a halt in the open country and you hear the lugubrious cry of an owl and the whining of a dog, the friends heard another voice, a sonorous voice addressing who knows whom and recounting something very distressing. And it was truly surprising to realize that that very distressing thing, recounted by that throbbing voice to who knows whom, was their own life.

The three friends promptly looked across at Buscaino, who was dozing in an armchair. There was the man who had saved them once, and would save them again and better! When his voice, loudly ringing in the guise of hammer-blows, began to make itself heard again, then the other, murmuring that gloomy tale, would all at once fall silent. Oh, if they hadn't had the idea and the energy to build the tower, how clear it was that Natàca would have quenched the three of them at a puff, like so many candle ends.

Yes, it was clear that Natàca was a deadly city. But there were three things in Natàca which were by no means clear.

One was the look in the eyes of Professor Luigini, which shone in an extraordinary way, so that one was compelled, like someone who has closed the shutters and turned off all the lights but still sees a ray of light on the floor, to wonder where on earth that light was coming from. The professor was a man of inveterate serenity and, although he was subject to tantrums and occasionally lost his temper, shouting and gesticulating, there was always a part of him which continued to smile. So also in his art. He wrote poems in dialect, and although these expressed doubts and afflictions not typical of men who think naturally in dialect, or of the times at which one does think in dialect, his verses were simpler, more sincere and enduring, than the words which of an evening escape the lips of peasants. How come?

A second thing was the way Maria Careni and her husband dealt with life. For on Sundays they would stroll along the avenues in the Public Gardens followed by a pram from the depths of which a tiny creature did not even minimally return the look which her sister, trotting beside the vehicle, kept constantly fixed on her, but stared instead with uncommon absorption at her little brother who, arm outstretched, clumsily opened and closed his fist in token of farewell while perched on the forearm of a tall, dark nursemaid. What was the meaning of their mania for snapshots, which led to every Sunday being preserved in hundreds of copies, and faces and objects (in which our three friends were disgusted to notice that, beneath that very Time which refused to budge, life fled away in a twinkling) were lovingly and painstakingly repeated on paper matt and glossy, and that if the diminutive Lello opened his mouth to ask for a balloon the fact was recorded in albums, on the walls, on the table-tops and above the head of their bed? And what was the attraction of that game in which the father and mother, seated on a bench, had the nanny poke the baby girl's face out at them through the foliage, and then would make her smile, first from a distance and then from close up, and then give her a scare but at once elicit a smile again?

All this was far from clear! Maybe just daft . . .

The third and last thing was the attitude of Giovanni's uncle.

That ruddy and chubby employee of the Customs and Excise had for thirteen years been listening to the conversations which, late in the evening, our friends were wont to hold in the dining-room. Well then, what did he think about it? To tell the truth, it was by no means certain that among the mysterious and pleasant events which occurred in that gentleman's inner being, concerning which for so many years he had thought it best to be secretive, there was necessarily any place for thought and adjudication. Nor was it right that the gloomier the talk of our friends the brighter his eyes sparkled, as if for him the thought of grief and misfortune was like the wind which out of doors can kill people and denude the trees, while indoors it fans up the fire and keeps the place warm. The man was very likely a moron, but a moron who was beginning to be suspect. They had to lure him out of his beatitude and see how he reacted.

So one evening Giovanni, Leonardo and Rodolfo broke off in the middle of their conversation and addressed him bluntly: what did he think? Was Natàca a miserable town, or wasn't it? And had they not had one hell of a struggle, to keep from being swallowed up by boredom and putrefaction?

Signor Roberto Luisi quaked in the face of these interrogations; disconcerted, he passed a hand across his brow. "Yes," he said, "no, yes, I mean yes, no . . ." But when he expressed the opinion that that was not quite the way things had gone the three of them so pinioned him with their arguments, hinted so darkly, and eventually told him outright that he wasn't up to understanding, the poor man's face blotched yellow and red and he was afflicted by a nervous yawn which try as he might he could not stop. He therefore got up, and with the doubtless childish excuse of going to his bedroom to fetch a handkerchief he left the dining-room and did not come back.

It really did seem that the arguments of the three friends had swept him away, like a bird that has been snug in the midst of a storm, but only because the wind has not yet seen fit to enter its nest. But the following day, propped against a glass in the middle of the table, the trio discovered a white envelope. Opening it, they found the following letter:

Dear boys,
 I'm not good at discussions, so yesterday I cut a rather sorry figure in your eyes. But in the night I bethought me of my old pen, rusty as it is, and I appealed to it to defend me worthily. So here I am, as Dante put it, *treading in the imprints of those cherished feet.*
 I persist in thinking that you've gone out of your minds. The time that's passing, the time that won't pass . . . What sort of idiocies are these? Personally, I have for thirty years been working modestly at the Customs and Excise, and many Natàcan men have worked modestly beside me. What is there to do, you ask? Why, there is work, and after that there's relaxation! Now there's a decent programme for an honest man! But you're a bunch of good-for-nothings. *Mercy and Justice hold you in contempt!* From what I gathered yesterday you think of life as an empty sack into which one has to chuck anything at all, even excrement, as long as one fills it. Instead of working according to the dictates of conscience and modesty (*Clear and decorous conscience, O to thee/What a grievous pang is a small offence*!) you divide your time between the most discreditable idleness and the most hare-brained schemes. *Thou art wise, And understandst me/better than I can speak.* One moment you think yourselves lame ducks, the next colossi, windbags even in this, now full now floppy, according to whether or not some loud noise comes along to inflate you. In short, during the thirteen years you've been living in Natàca what have you actually *done*?

"What have we done?" yelled Rodolfo, beside himself. "What have we *done*?"
 He stalked to the window, raised a lace curtain, held it up with his left hand and, turning to his friends and flourishing his

right, indicated, outside the window behind him, the darkness which contained the panoramic tower. "*That's* what we've done!" he exclaimed.

By an extraordinary coincidence the tower was at that instant illuminated by the searchlight of a ship anchored in the harbour in the east.

"Look!" cried Leonardo. "It's all lit up!"

They all three stared in wonder and excitement. After a while the searchlight ceased to focus on the green cone and turned to scan the clouds. Against the dark sky the tall stem of the tower was now a dingy colour, like the unlit part of the moon during the first quarter.

"Anyway," said Giovanni, "my uncle is a rotten sod. I don't want to clap eyes on him again. Either he leaves this house or I do. My father will have to choose: it's either him or me!"

This said, he was seized by a fit of rage, or by a strong desire to do something outlandish but at the same time perfectly appropriate. What, in fact? Well, we are ashamed to admit it, but it was his habit as a child to throw himself on the ground in order to alter his parents' "no" to "yes"; and now it resurfaced. And the funny part is that in the thirty-five years which had followed his first five, there had been no change in his character to prevent him from indulging such a desire. It rose, it rose from the very depths of his instincts, and who knows in what part of the room he would have hurled himself down if he had not at that moment heard the telephone ring, and shortly afterwards Buscaino on the wire loudly announcing that the shareholders had come up with the last instalment, that the last line of defence had fallen, and victory was at the gates.

"God," cried Rodolfo, "God has seen fit to punish that old rotter at once! We'll throw our money in his face! Even a man of his type will have respect for banknotes! And he won't use the word hare-brained of a business that in a few months earns hundreds, yes, several little hundreds of little thousands of lire!"

IV

THE GREEN CONE, fashioned in the Moorish style, rested on nine slender columns. The architrave beneath the terrace was painted gold, and the frieze, a pattern of elongated spheres, a glittering sea-green. The window of the second floor was triangular, flawlessly picked out by its three-sided decoration and topped by a rosette. Its sill was rounded, with a corbel consisting of a large, carved stone knot terminating in a tassel. The first and third storeys were pierced to east and west by half-moon-shaped windows which, being in opposite walls and without either shutters or glass, were like the images from two eyes meeting in the mind. The ample spirals of the staircase draped themselves around the walls. Climbing them one received the impression of treading on a sky about to crack like ice . . . But a person mounting them that evening need no longer halt either at the first floor or the second – he could go all the way up to the terrace; for the staircase had been completed and the tower needed nothing further from the masons' hammers.

Buscaino, seated on the top step, was looking down over the panorama of Natàca spread at his feet, over those thousands of roofs that cloaked a way of life which Buscaino knew from long and bitter experience. One of those roofs sheltered Duke Fausto Villadora, another Cavaliere De Filippi, another Nereggia, yet another Sugarloaf Maled, and a fifth Avvocato De Marchi; every roof in sight had its bigwig and its Hooligan to shelter. And then those terraces where the washing, quivering in the slight breeze, seemed in sign language to be asking "What shall we do this evening?"; and the streets like cracks between the roofs, at the bottom of which a black-clad host, at every step it took, must needs unstick its footsoles from the ground. All this, seen from a height, was on the brink of pronouncing a very clear and poignant statement, like the bed in which an invalid, after a ten-year confinement, sees the imprint of his own body. Eastward was the sea, raising up dinghies and steamships alike until they touched the sky, whence now and again a black speck slid by degrees down into the jaws of the harbour. To the south the golden sands grew dim and vanished in the dusk of distance beneath the ash-grey hills, while to the north the Mountain loomed, broad and lofty, but so blue that it seemed that stars must soon begin to peep from it, as from any other part of the sky. And through the sky there advanced towards Buscaino two white clouds like a huge book open on a lectern and borne towards him by the angels of twilight; the great book of life in which, just as soon as the words became legible, he would read that the Lord blessed him, in both past and future, for what he had undergone and what he had brought to pass.

The bounty of the Lord rained copiously up here, chilling the shoulders. Only a peevish soul would call it the damp.

Buscaino would have dearly liked to weep. But that same joy which drew the tears from his heart stopped them from welling over, as if these were the tears worthy of a man who has suffered and won, a weeping of the breast, inward and invisible, very different from the tears that stream from the eyes and trickle into the mouth. Yes, he had suffered. To Rodolfo, sitting on a lower step, and tilting back his head to look up at him, he revealed things that only victory can wring from a man of dignity . . . That one can go for five or six days without a bite to eat: verily, in such cases, the Heavenly Father puts nutritive value into the fumes from grill-room doorways or the odour of steak on the breath of a friend. Debts can be attended to without undue inconvenience: the secret lies in keeping one's creditors' faces at a safe distance. But heavens alive! these thrusting men of business, how *can* they take such delight in having their photos taken? The photographers' shop-windows had gradually filled up with the faces of his creditors. One of the latter, hung over the wickerwork table, the only one they usually set outside the Prince Café, used to glare down on milk or ice-cream alike with such a look of Creditor that more than once Buscaino was obliged to relinquish the contents of the cup or dish before him. And what about his hair? It might seem an easy thing to find the two lire you need for a haircut. Not so, however. Those two lire play harder to get than in a field ringed by hills is a wind to strip the trees of their dead leaves. And the proof is Buscaino's Americanly close-cropped head now almost invisible in so luxuriant a black fleece of curls. "I swear to you," he said, "I can no longer tell where to find my brains."

This tickled Rodolfo, and he laughed.

"Laugh away, laugh away," said Buscaino. "Up here we have the right to laugh. We have the duty to be optimists. And to forgive."

And forgiveness and good feeling were distributed by Buscaino like wine to the guests at the wedding feasts of the rich. The staircase was all a coming-and-going of Hooligans and persons of every rank and station. The former left their footmarks on the steps in a paste so malodorous that on a day of ill humour one might well wonder whether they didn't spend their whole time in the wake of a cow. Down below was Tommasini holding the hand of his small son, one of the saddest creatures ever born – the world's favourite looking-glass, as Buscaino used to say in his moments of deepest dejection: at the age of five he already knew the art of beating his head against a brick wall. Tommasini was waving to Buscaino with wide sweeps of his free arm, as a faithful soldier might at the Flag when finally hoisted atop an enemy fortress.

But who were these characters demanding room to pass and behaving as if they owned the place, treading first on Rodolfo's hat and then on Buscaino's jacket? Indulgence needed here! . . .

From the pocket of one of these there fluttered a sheet of paper which could well have been an excerpt from the foremost epic poem of Natàca, to such heights had poetic style and the dark reveries of this town been therein raised. The page read as follows:

> Then these people transformed into spirits are under orders to transform all those who enter these woods.
>
> All those who have perished in landslides and avalanches are consigned to the caverns and have the same powers as the former.
>
> All those who are drowned have the same power, the same might as the others, but they have rights of surveillance over the entire French Royal Navy.
>
> These spirits may not absent themselves without the command of their chief.
>
> When one of these spirits succeeds in escaping and becomes assimilated into a person, the latter feels a kind of dizziness and the spirit changes itself into a tapeworm and renders the person tubercular. These spirits also incorporate themselves in animals.
>
> When these spirits go forth in groups by command of their chief, they are under orders to destroy ships, and the majority of such cases will occur in the years 3000 and 4000, the which by command of Santa Genoveffa.

Forgiven, even this is forgiven! Buscaino stood up and slowly made his way down the steps. Forgiven, forgiven and even admired! . . .

Ah, the power of victory over social relations! One who has had a bit of success becomes tolerant towards his neighbour; the latter, now tolerated, in gratitude becomes more charming and tolerable; both would for a while follow the path of mutual love were it not that, scared by excess, even of benevolence, the former did not take it into his head to despise the latter, and the latter to envy the former.

The following day was a Tuesday. Five days to go until the great celebration with dinner and dancing on the second floor of the tower. Buscaino entrusted his head to the hands of a barber. The young fellow snipped and snapped his scissors for two hours but Buscaino's head never came to light, as when one has stripped and nibbled nearly all the leaves from an artichoke but cannot find the heart. Buscaino himself, who was watching in the mirror and from the very fact that he thought he no longer had a head could deduce that he must still have one, was no less worried than the barber. At last it was seen that the artichoke did have a heart to it, but so skinny and small! Buscaino's head had been overworked and reduced by the anxieties of life in Natàca. Farewell to its erstwhile charms! The child's face which won first prize in the beauty competition for the offspring of civic employees, and which still smiled in a small snapshot he kept in his wallet, would have had much fault to find with this other face, successor to the same name and set on the same neck, forty-five years later.

"We can't keep the promises we made as children," thought Buscaino. "I, for example, swore that as a man I would be handsome, placid, plump and judicious. Huh! But we've forgiven so many people that we can surely be indulgent towards ourselves. Besides, I made no promise then that I would provide Natàca with a panoramic tower, and instil such a go-ahead spirit into these listless people. So, no regrets – let's laugh instead!"

A photograph of Buscaino, taken the previous day and now on show in a shop-window, wore a smile of victory in the midst of the worried expressions of his creditors, which ever since the summer had been gradually yellowing before the eyes of the passers-by.

This winter was dry and sparkling. But the men most in the public eye had all bought eskimo-type fur overcoats, and thus swathed and swollen they strolled in the almost springlike sunshine. Pursuing another fashion imported from the North, those who were not wrapped in such voluminous fur overcoats were wearing ones with wide padded shoulders, so that an air of robustness circulated among the youth of Natàca. This by no means displeased Buscaino. Joy is like a thinking seed; and what would a seed be thinking an hour, a bare hour after touching the soil? That it had given birth to trees already tall. Thus Buscaino's joy imagined that because he had bestowed such a victory on Natàca the city was already more flourishing, more self-confident, and that its young men were growing up more sturdy . . .

"Does Sunday's invitation include even me?" Buscaino was accosted by Lisa Careni, holding a little girl by the hand.

"Signorina, it is I who should ask *you* whether *I* am invited!" replied he.

"Oh, how gallant, how gallant! I almost forgive you for having been the ruin of Leonardo."

"The ruin of Leonardo? Signorina, this is something new to me, indeed it is. And why am I supposed to have been the ruin of Leonardo?"

"Because the poor chap would have discovered that his life was not sane and serious, and would certainly have done something about it if you, my dear professor, had not given him the illusion that his life had found a purpose in this tower business."

"Tower business! You've put your finger on it. This tower business – and what a business! Thousands and thousands of lire! Moreover, have I not silenced your most vexing question: what shall we do this evening? Come off it, my dear Lisa! Anyway, get yourself up like a dream. There'll be a lot of light in the tower on Sunday evening, and not a hair on your head but must be divinely beautiful. You promise?"

"I promise," said Lisa, shaking him by the hand and going on her way with the little girl (who had vaguely gathered, from what she had heard, something that her own mother – herself at that time also in short skirts and towelling panties – must have vaguely gathered from just such a conversation: that while growing up in Natàca she would have to put a lot of effort into finding something to do, especially in the evenings).

Buscaino, however, was rubbing his hands with glee. In every shop he left a visiting card, with the most diverse orders but only the one address. Many refined objects, including flowers and candles, would be moving on Sunday morning in the direction of the tower. Only the light was tardy in coming, just like Leonardo's. The electric light wires had not yet honoured the panoramic tower with their presence. Buscaino telephoned every half-hour, and each time learnt that a workman with a ladder had set off for the tower five minutes earlier. There was also the official permit to open the tower to the public, which had not yet been issued. But it soon would be.

V

Soon, my foot! An appalling communication cut Buscaino's legs from under him as with an axe. A shrimp of a hunchback in a green uniform had called and consigned to Rodolfo a document bearing three rubber stamps, in which it was stated that Professor Buscaino was "liable to a fine and up to five years' imprisonment should he contravene the order, hereby issued, not to open the tower to the public." The building commission was of the opinion that the structure of the edifice was very unsound and the exterior staircase treacherous and unstable. For the above reasons, and for a third, perhaps more serious still but not explained, the Town Hall gave instructions "that the public be kept away from such an unsafe place."

"No!" cried Buscaino. "It's a nightmare dreamt up by petty clerks and pen-pushers! A horrendous outcome of the sedentary life! Nothing in this document is remotely human. I must tear off at once to the Town Hall. Just you watch – I'll wake up those calamitous mummies! Even there I'll restore some sense of reality!"

So Buscaino tore off to the Town Hall. A youth with a face that would have been one big smile had not there tarried about his nose – and specifically in the groove inflicted by the clips of his eye-glasses – an air of solemn gravity glanced at the document which Buscaino held shakingly before him and jerked his chin at a door on the left down the passage.

Buscaino tore up to that door, opened it a fraction, poked his head in and cast his eye around. Amidst piles of papers, stacks of registers, tables, typewriters, pens and pencils, he descried a man. Within this man, though at an infinite distance, like a rowing-boat viewed through the wrong end of a telescope, he also descried some grey-matter which, at last overcoming the difficulties and uncertainties of focusing from miles away, became aware that a head was sticking in through the doorway, deduced that there was a person attached to it, and, smiling a crafty smile as if to say "You can't fool me, I know you're not a disembodied head floating around in mid-air like a balloon, you're nothing more nor less than a member of the public," muttered something which Buscaino optimistically interpreted as "Come in".

Buscaino stepped in and closed the door behind him. The little man raised his head from the paper over which he bent with his whole body and weighed on with his elbows, and riveted his eyes on Buscaino's face as though seeking there the phrase his pen was in need of. Buscaino very patiently bore the dead weight of that stare, and indeed he lowered it as far as he could by making a long, deep bow. Maybe he cherished the hope that bowing his head would cause the stare to slide off onto the floor and that the resulting jar would waken it; but on straightening up Buscaino saw those eyes were still on his face, still misty and engrossed in their search.

"Begging your pardon, sir," began Buscaino, "but I am the Professor Buscaino to whom the worshipful Town Hall yesterday sent this document which, with your permission, I venture to consider, I will not say scarcely justified, but based on information that is inexact and perhaps even not unbiassed."

The little man began to put his desk in order, stacking up manuscripts on his right, typescripts on his left, and placing the inkpot in the middle. Then, seeing that it was not quite dead centre, he shifted it ever so little and laid his pen across the neck of it.

"Yes?"

"Begging your pardon, sir, I am appealing to you to obtain justice in this thoroughly muddled business."

"What business?"

"The business of the panoramic tower, concerning which the Town Hall sent me the document which . . . This is it, sir."

The little man took the paper and, since it was typed, stacked it up on the left.

"If your Worship would care to look at it . . ."

The clerk shot it a covert glance, with the air of someone throwing a stone into space and immediately averting his gaze.

"If you would care to read it, I was saying . . ."

"Read it?"

"Yes, read it."

"But I wrote the thing myself!"

"Heaven be praised! But begging your pardon sir, how did such intelligence and expertise as yours come to issue such an injunction, which by your leave I venture to define as not altogether just, or at least not as perfectly just as all the other injunctions issued by your Worship?"

"Yes, I wrote that document myself . . ."

"Yes sir, I have grasped that. But why?"

"Why what?"

"Look here sir, how *can* I be forbidden, after such heavy expenses, after ten years of sweat and blood, how *can* I be forbidden to open the panoramic tower to the public?"

"Ah . . . Ah, I see. You've come about the matter of the tower?"

"Dear God above," thought Buscaino, "remember, if only for a single minute, what you promised this man when you had him born a man, and not a horse or a mouse!" Aloud he said, "Yes indeed, sir, I have come about the matter of the tower. What else had you understood, your Worship?"

"Understood! . . ."

(In point of fact, with regard to this last utterance not even the author knows whether it should be written as above, or not rather as "Understood?").

"Yes sir, the tower!"

"Look here, we sent you an injunction. Where is it?"

"But your Worship, it's there on your desk. That's it!"

The clerk picked up the document which he had stacked on his left and, after a cursory glance, placed it to his right. Then, realizing this was hardly proper, replaced it on his left.

"An injunction," he said. "A ban on opening the tower to the public."

"Your Worship," Buscaino hastened to say like one who, the person inside refusing to open, has battered at a door for an hour and seeing a chink in it hurls himself forward even at the risk of getting crushed, "your Worship, believe me, this ban is unjustified, absurd, inhuman. I've worked for ten years! There are huge sums of money involved. This is no childish fun and games. The outside staircase is as solid as a rock, I assure you. In any case, if need be we'll reinforce it. Your Worship, I beg you!"

A few minutes later the little man's face lit up, as if at last he had heard something.

"You will reinforce the outside staircase?"

"Yes, your Worship. And I am willing to act in person as a caryatid, and support it on my own shoulders, rather than see my work go to waste, and in such a manner."

A few more minutes' silence; and then the little man's face lit up again, and with the usual start, as if struck without warning by a word and its meaning, he exclaimed, "Your work you say?"

"Great God on high!" thought Buscaino once more. "What do I think I'm talking to?"

Indeed, though at first sight there were only two persons in the room, one of them talking and the other listening and answering, there must really have been a third person, one who registered what Buscaino shouted, then began to walk solemnly round the room five or six times with those words in his mind and finally, in a very modest and courteous voice proceeded to garble Buscaino's words into the ear of the little clerk; who suddenly heard, then digested them, and then replied.

"O Natàca the Sluggish!" thought Buscaino. "Here more sluggish than ever: here I am in the very heart of your sluggishness."

"Now then," queried the little clerk. "What is it you want?"

"What do I want, sir? Justice, that's what!"

Two minutes' silence.

"But this is the Town Hall!"

"Yes, I am aware this is not the Law Courts. But is not the Town Hall also the seat of just and benevolent actions?"

Two minutes' silence.

"Professor Buscaino, it is not simply a matter of the unsafe staircase."

"Thank heaven for that! Then what is it a matter of?"

One minute's silence.

"It is forbidden to admit the public to high places from which persons who mean ill, lunatics you understand, who do not realize the importance of life, might . . ."

"Might what, sir?"

"Throw themselves off."

"Commit suicide, you mean?"

"Yes, suicide."

"But your Honour, if you prohibit me from opening the tower to the public, from reaping the fruits of my ten years' work, of my sweat and my blood, and from paying my debts, what other citizen of Natàca could possibly think of throwing himself from a height of a hundred and fifty feet if not I myself, your Worship, I and nobody else?"

Two minutes' silence.

"Well, you have a right . . ."

"Ah yes? I have a right to kill myself? Has the municipality no injunction for the safeguarding of my life?"

One minute's silence.

"You are the owner of the tower, and the municipality cannot deprive you of your right to enter your own property."

"Enter it in my present state of mind, and it'll mean an exit of a quite different sort. If I enter at the bottom I shall exit from the top!"

The little man began hunting for a paper. His fingers, without the aid of his eyes but raising their tips like tiny heads, sniffed here and there for the presence of that document, which was evidently of capital importance; they twisted this way and that, they plunged in among the old papers and finally, coming up with a small yellow rectangle, handed it to Buscaino.

The latter, from the mere form and colour of it, the way in which it trembled in the little man's fingers, the coats of arms with which it was embellished, the rubber stamps with which it was covered, felt that his misfortune was ineluctable, that the injunction issued against him was of almost divine origin. Substantially, the document stated that it was forbidden, absolutely forbidden, to admit the public to elevated places such as panoramic towers, skyscrapers etc., because experience shows that these soon become an incentive to suicide and a means of committing it.

"But since when?" cried Buscaino. "Since when?"

This question surprised the little man, who was a thousand miles away from the whole matter of the tower; a matter which, consequent on the appearance of that rectangle of paper, he considered to be completely closed.

"When did this ban come into force?"

The clerk took his time about returning the thousand miles back to the subject, then stated:

"Fourteen years ago."

"Fourteen years ago?" gasped Buscaino. "Fourteen years!"

For a moment he stood bewildered. Then, without so much as a word to the little man, he seized his hat and rushed out.

On the staircase a voice murmured, "Professor, I ought not to be doing this, and in fact I'm going against my duty. But friendship's a duty too . . . Take care. There's a whole crowd of bailiffs out with orders to track you down. And it's not unlikely they'll hand matters over to the police. Maybe you'd better take a change of air . . ."

"Thanks!" said Buscaino, without turning to see who was speaking into his ear. He ran down the stairs.

No sooner outside but his eye fell on the tower, and immediately his thoughts returned to that yellowed document, as when one part of our mind remembers our old friend Tom as we saw him last, young, happy and full of life, while the other dwells on the telegram which has this moment told us of his death.

"So," thought Buscaino, "we work, we struggle, we sweat blood, we raise stone upon stone, and finally we think we have built something useful and durable; but hidden beneath a pile of registers is a small sheet of yellowed paper: half a dozen little words, an inviolable law, something that pops up at the last moment and informs us that our work is an offence, that we have been working in a direction not only mistaken but forbidden. Quite so. But in what direction have I devoted all my efforts if not heavenwards? Can such a direction be mistaken? If so, why not tell us to aim towards the centre of the earth, towards hell and the devil! . . ." His head was spinning. He leant it against a shop window.

"The heavens, the devil . . . Isn't it time I stopped talking like a madman? Now that I'm really on the verge of madness, wouldn't it be better to think and speak more modestly, more reasonably? And what about the debts? O God! God help me!"

Buscaino sat down on the balustrade in front of the shop and permitted his poor emaciated body to faint away.

VI

On windy evenings the twinkling of the planet Jupiter fills the whole sky of the South, as if the wind were blowing at it and it alone, making it blaze. In little rooms where the thrifty hand of woman can never bring itself to switch on the light, Jupiter sends its mild and tremulous rays, and glitters in the mirrors. Admittedly it is not the sun, it is not the moon. No one has ever said "What a lovely Jupiter-lit night!" But the eyes of the women of the South love this silvery light that barely touches the earth but seems forever on the point of illuminating it.

That evening even the eyes of Buscaino (for though he was not a woman his recent misfortunes had aroused something of the feminine in him) . . . through the windows of the reception room on the second floor of the tower even the eyes of Buscaino were fixed upon the planet Jupiter.

Warned in time, the Electricity Company had not seen fit to risk the expense of installing a system in the panoramic tower, of throwing away money on the House of Bankruptcy. It could therefore be said that the reception room was in the dark, unless one bestowed excessive importance on the candle which, caught by gusts of wind, twisted this way and that its tiny tip of flame.

The lighting had not arrived. But the provisions, the flowers, the sweetmeats, the fruit, all these had closed in like great Birnam Wood to high Dunsinane Hill. In vain had Buscaino sought to keep the stuff in the shops, sending round notes in which he vigorously countermanded his orders. The grocers, the greengrocers, the butchers had replied, "The stuff's already sold. Do what you like with it. We're not keeping it here!"

Kids with that beseeching look still in their eyes, "dead man's bones", apples, pears, gherkins, cakes, fish, salamis, cheeses, chickens, partridges and a multitude of fragrant things had come to the tower and found their place in a corner of the reception room. In spite of everything Buscaino had decided to have a small supper, just the few of them: Giovanni, Leonardo, Rodolfo, Tommasini and himself. The agreed hour was nine o'clock. But it was already half-past, and Buscaino saw no sign of his fellow diners.

The wind outside was growing wilder. The hanging streetlamps swung jerkily to and fro, casting shadows which raced across walls and roofs. Sometimes they even turned upside down, and their rays struck the dome of the cathedral, and the sword of the stone angel spat forth a dazzle . . . Down below, in the garden round the tower, the trees crashed one against the other, and the sound the leaves made might have been a shriek. Up there, the windows rattled, the flame of the candle was blown clear off the wick, and the whole tower felt as if it were leaning very slowly over to the left. As in fact it was. When the wind struck the tower the left of the window revealed a new constellation, while the right frame hid half the light of the planet Jupiter. When the great gust subsided, Jupiter reappeared in its entirety and the stars on the left were hidden again.

Ten years of life thrown away down there in that pit of black houses! Ten years in those chairs, in those beds on those floors!

Buscaino sat himself down at the head of the table.

"Lord," he began, "I do not ask You to undo what is done, or that Natàca should give me back my youth, or that the tower should be opened to the public. I only ask that I should see the funny side, in the end find something to laugh at in all this, like the dog that at last swallows the fly which has been preventing it from sleeping. If You wish, I'll scale down my desires, and be modest, even if modesty itself might seem an offence to Your omnipotence . . . So really all I ask is for someone to come and keep me company!"

But no one came. And among the heap of provisions, whence pears and cakes and flowers sent forth their fragrance, the staring eyes of the dead beasts were in no way appetizing; they begged for aid quite other than the good offices of sauce or of salad; they did not make the mouth water; they appealed to the heart with that bewildered look, you know not whether accusing or compassionate, whether seeing nothing or more than you do: the look that is always there in the eyes of the dead.

At last the sound of footsteps is heard on the stairs outside, now to right and now to left, according to the spiralling of the steps; now clear and now faint, according to the wind; a sound bearing someone up. Now he is in the lobby, now in the doorway. Rodolfo De Mei, umbrella in hand, stops for a moment to peer into the semi-darkness, then throws down his overcoat with a brusque gesture and moves up to the table.

Buscaino realized at once that his friend, stock-still beside the table, was possessed by a single thought, nay, less than a thought – by a single word. As soon as Rodolfo opened his mouth he was apprised that the word was "Quite!"

"Are you perhaps a little late?"

"Quite!"

"But Leonardo and Giovanni aren't here yet."

"Quite."

"Are you holding something against me?"

With a visible effort Rodolfo choked back his one and only word, and said nothing.

"What is it you're holding against me?"

With an even more laborious effort Rodolfo gave up on that word, spoken or unspoken, and with some difficulty adopted others: "A fine finale, this!"

Now it was Buscaino's turn to answer, "Quite."

"And you didn't half make us a few promises!"

"Ah, come off it, Rodolfo, don't take it that way. You know

perfectly well that the tower couldn't be opened to the public because of the staircase . . ."

"Buscaino, let's face facts: the staircase is just a pretext. You know the real reason for this ban is altogether different."

"I agree. But is that my fault?"

"Is that your fault? Isn't it yours, this tower project?"

"The project is mine, but you carried it out, and with considerable zest too!"

"I believed you to be a man, and a heaven-sent man at that. I imagined that the project of such a man would be well thought out, reliable, serviceable, something to make people talk about us in years to come."

"Nor were you mistaken, Rodolfo. You will indeed be talked about in years to come. The tower can't be erased like a child's scribble on a slate. The tower is here to stay. They may say anything about us except that we have not done a job of work!"

"Quite! But what people will actually say is that there were so many useful little jobs to be done, and those wastrels (wastrels, us!) chose to dream up something as grandiose, exacting and absurd as this. And you've made us work for ten years – ten years, mark you! – on such a brainless scheme."

"My scheme was not brainless, Rodolfo, and it was not absurd. If I think back to the moment when I was in the train crossing the viaduct overlooking Natàca, and first conceived the idea for the panoramic tower, well, I find nothing abnormal or reprehensible about the young Buscaino of that moment. Everything was in order, everything was as it should be in the little man who decided to invest the precious capital of his own energy in the dilatory working ways and niggardly money of Natàca. But the truth is that this is a grim, God-blighted land, and there's no good seed that can rightly prosper in it. The most sensible and practical idea, sown among a people which includes Leopoldi, discoverer of perpetual motion, Nereggia the author of Morreale, Sugarloaf Maled the king of England, etc. etc., is inevitably destined to bear crazy fruit."

"So then, your idea of a panoramic tower, put into practice

three years after the ban on building panoramic towers, was a sensible one? Really, I don't know what to think of you."

"My dear Rodolfo, let's leave that aside. The fact remains that you have thought well of me for ten years, have you not? And now you think ill of me."

"Yes, it's quite a jolt!"

Quite a jolt indeed! How can one, after ten years of thinking well of Buscaino, suddenly turn round and think ill of him? It seems a small matter, like turning over a page in a book, but it isn't. Rodolfo had realized that his life was linked by a thousand threads to the fact of thinking well of Buscaino. And now he had been forced to admit that even the tiny robin red-breast (the robin, be it said, as he saw it then, with its unworried little head and its song like the sound of two stones tapped together, as if those warblings were not merely beautiful, but useful, not merely music but work), that even the robin had been linked by a thread to thinking well of Buscaino. When that thread snapped the robin deteriorated into a tiresome bird with a tap-tapping song that apes the sound of workmen hammering stone and building useless towers. And then the warning signal proceeding from the discovery that the man in whom he had placed most trust was a poor crackpot; the signal to bring reason to the defence of the sheeplike heart which, having once decided to trust blindly in one thing (rather than put that pampered blindness at risk), decides to trust in everything without distinction; the signal to reopen his eyes, to think for himself, to entertain doubts – this summoned him back to an exertion that was scarcely bearable after ten years of disuse.

"Think ill of you? Switching from the idea I had of you until yesterday to the one I am bound to have of you tomorrow, I feel as if someone were thrusting their hands into my flesh and wrenching my skeleton back to front. I'm on the rack!"

"Rodolfo, I don't know what to say to you . . . You rather overstepped the mark when you threw yourself lock, stock and barrel into the panoramic tower project. No one asked so much of you. You could have done other jobs at the same time . . .

Impossible, for me. I had to give myself to that project body and soul. And so I did. And here I am, ruined! Who will now give me back my ten lost years? My creditors want their money. But what will happen if when one of them says to me 'I want my thousand back,' I reply, 'And you give me back the fine days of my forties. Make the first figure of my age a four again!'"

"I simply can't imagine how you still have the effrontery to play the fool!"

Buscaino adopted a different tone.

"What do you want from me, Rodolfo, for God's sake? What do you want from me? I was on the brink of madness. I'll say more: I tried to go mad! Having realized that the sun was beginning to look to me like any other object, that I no longer made any distinction between the tumbler at my fingertips on the bedside table and the bright disk that (yes!) I might well pluck from the window, then I sat down on the bed and waited for everything to reach its consummation, for my eyes to go all staring and my brains to go phut. I was already smiling at the thought of leaving an insane Buscaino on the hands of my creditors – a stuffed doll who would pay them all back – but with gusts of laughter. I hoped that the memory of the tower would vanish from my mind, and that two and two would at last make five. Some hope, my dear Rodolfo! Two and two continued to make four, no more and no less, and the image of the tower did not budge an inch. I was forced to concede that I was still in my right mind. And listen to this one: I sought out Tommasini, who as you know is a flawless fabricator of madness – he's often played dirty tricks on my sanity. I placed myself in his hands, I allowed him to pull my leg in every possible way, I responded to that level gaze of his that beckons one to madness as to a haven of peace, with the thought: 'Let's hope it works!' . . . But it was all in vain, Rodolfo, and here I still am, having to render account for myself, for you, for the tower, for my debts. And in a short while, when I blow out the candle, I may well have a gloomy thought, but there's no doubt of it's being a sane and natural one."

"Sane? At the cost of being left in the dark, I'd be curious to see you blow out that candle and hear this sane thought of yours. It would be your first ever!"

"You're bitter, Rodolfo! But I have already been punished enough!"

"In all that has happened there's only one bright spark for me, and when I've told you it I'll go. It's this: that even you, who thought of yourself as some sort of earthquake or other, have stayed on in Natàca like the rest of us. Caught in the trap! Good-bye!"

Rodolfo slammed the door behind him so violently that the candle did blow out. The window now became a crowd of stars in a sky of which the deep, calm light would have brought great comfort, had it not been for the wind that swayed it slowly to right and to left, as if not even the sky had a right to be quiet and still.

And the odd thing is that the wind was not satisfied with this lofty achievement. Like someone whose hands play a violin worthy of the angels while his foot beats time on a cracked drum, so the wind, at the same time as swaying the sky and its stars, bowled through the streets of Natàca an old rusty basin, or something more squalid still. The streets of Natàca! The stairs of Natàca! There Buscaino had left the very best of himself, the most dynamic decade of his life. Now along those streets, past those lava-built walls and decrepit doorways, the wind was rolling a rattle of old tin, a sound half comic, half piteous. Whence came this sound? Really from a tin basin? Was it not rather from the chunk of his life he had left out there, left down in Natàca, left to the mercy of the wind? And as a wounded man abandoned by night in open country feels that hyenas have seized upon his severed leg and are rolling it with their claws, away along the path and into some ditch, some dry stream-bed, making sad moan in the streets of Natàca Buscaino heard that chunk of his life, those ten lost, cherished years, rolling over and over in the claws of the savagest wind that ever visited the city.

All of a sudden he thought: "What if those ten years were to become twenty? What if, on the spur of the moment, instead of imagining things, I should fling my own corpse into the claws of this Natàcan wind? What if I have really fallen into this trap for ever?"

He went to the window and looked out over the few lamps of Natàca scattered between one blackness and another. He was conscious of their looking back at him sleepily and without concern, like the eyes a sentry turns towards his prisoner when the latter is firmly bound and in no position to escape.

"Ah no! No! No!"

He rushed out, leapt down the steps. There was an old church-hen who had been promised the job of caretaker and who slept in a hut near the tower. On her door he hammered.

"Who's there?" demanded the woman, huddled up in a kind of mattress.

"Get your handbag and come with me."

"Holy mother of God, what's happened?" she babbled. But no time to think twice before she was already on the second floor of the tower, hugging a dilapidated handbag, her shift billowing in the wind from the half-open door, her hair flying in all directions; and slipping and sliding, elbowed back into place, the wafer-thin mattress she used as a blanket.

"My good woman, these suckling lambs, these salamis, these cakes and all this fruit are worth a thousand lire. I'm offering you the lot for a hundred!"

"Lambs? Real live lambs?"

"Not alive, lucky devils! But freshly butchered. Good lady, it's a bargain. Let me have a hundred lire and may the Lord come to lunch with you!"

"But whatever shall I do with it all?"

"Granny, I've simply got to get away. Be good and open your bag. I tell you what, I'll open it for you. It works like this . . . Out comes a hundred-lire note . . . That's the way!"

The woman clutched one corner of the banknote with trembling fingers.

"Dear lady, this means a spree for you, and for me it means a railway ticket! Be a dear and forgive me. The stuff's all yours. And I bequeath you the tower into the bargain. God's blessings on your reverend head!"

At which Buscaino gave a sharp tug at the note, the woman a kiss on the forehead, and fled out leaving the door agape. The old thing was at a loss to know if the note had been snatched by a kind-hearted madcap or a thief who had simply made off with her money. Thus, havering between motherly feelings and calling the police, she stirred and lifted the tiny lambs with her foot, stroked their cold muzzles, sized up the salamis and cakes. Then she heaved a sigh and, adjusting the mattress round her shoulders, went out into the wild dark air and back to her dwelling.

VII

THE WIND MADE LIFE in Natàca no more cheerful. On the contrary, it seemed that having laid hands on the phrases "What a bore!" and "What shall we do this evening?" it was wafting them round the chimney-stacks and corridors of Natàca, carrying them a hundred, a thousand times to the same room, tucking them under the carpets or inside the neglected pianofortes and guitars, the strings of which, struck by the wind, in deep tones vibrated: "What a bore!" "What shall we do this evening?"

It appeared moreover that the tower was an unrivalled attraction for this wind, which roared around it, striking it right, striking it left, attempting to uproot it, knock it down, hammer it in, screw it in; contenting itself in the end with filling it with a long, melancholy moan.

In the streets the tiny men moved as on the palm of a hand that swept them swiftly along until, throwing open a café door, they made a headlong entry looking like schoolboys booted out of class. The girls kept close by the walls, the hems of their skirts fastened with ill-concealed clothes-pegs, their hands splayed about their knees. Hats and dead leaves skimmed along the ground, soared through the air, came to rest on balconies. A popular story was the one about Leopoldi, who for half an hour chased after the leaf of a plane-tree under the impression that it was his hat. "Put a crease in it!" yelled a street-arab the second the poor man succeeded in getting a foot onto the scrap of foliage that had caused him to run so far. Poor Leopoldi! That very evening he was discovered stock-still beside his wireless, while a cavernous voice filled his unhearing ear with encouraging phrases: "Strong, great, invincible . . . Impetus, power, toughness, tenacity, daring . . ." Poor Leopoldi. So still, so eternally still was he, the discoverer of perpetual motion. But of all those who came a cropper because of the wind, Leopoldi was the only one who never rose again. The rest concluded their adventure with a couple of flicks to dust off their knees or their backsides.

The worst of it was that the wind refused to let up. And the biggest complainer of all was the costermonger, who heard his fine voice (cracking up his lettuces) torn from his lips to boom out over his rival's barrow; or worse still, over the open carriage (drawn up at the kerb, two pretty, much got-up customers within it, throwing glances and greetings to all and sundry), which was discomfited by the words "Come buy these luscious lettuces!"

The landowners were full of complaints too, as they sniffed on the wind an over-strong scent of lemons, and were obliged to think that if the scent had come so far the fruit was unlikely to have remained on the branch.

But the poets did not complain. Those windy mornings the public gardens of Natàca were one continuous, enjoyable, beflustered burst of laughter. In this cheery sound they moved like atoms on the breath in the song of a happy young girl. They made their way along the avenues grabbing here at a treetrunk, there at a marble pillar. Laughter buffeted them to right and to left, they were filled and inflated with it. Changing suddenly to a wilder note, it shoved them roughly onto a bench. But no matter – what a joke! A little hard on the backside perhaps, but still a joke. The laughter grew cheerily friendly again, drawing sounds and words from this side and that, whirling them into the air and confusing them, so that the worthy ears of Nereggia and Cavallero, in the midst of so much confusion, plainly distinguished the lines respectively of their "Santa Genoveffa" and their "Santa Rita", more beautiful than they had ever been before, more forceful and adult than they were themselves, almost unrecognizable, like a son who suddenly confides to his unassuming father, "Dear dad, I have something to tell you. I am a god!" Ah then, then the threadbare coat, the wife's harsh words still ringing in the ear along with the slam of the door . . . then one's own name – never pronounced by many, and never with much respect by the few – then all becomes charming and delightful, as does the memory of the long wait in the ante-chamber when the door finally opens and you are ushered into the presence of the king . . . And who cares now whether they rest after lunch with their feet higher than their heads or vice versa. It no longer matters even if there will be no other lunch to follow that lunch, and no dinner either.

Full of this gale and these thoughts, Nereggia, Cavallero and De Filippi roved the Public Gardens. But they were not alone, as on other stormy days. Rodolfo De Mei, umbrella in hand, had also come out to the sound of the oleanders and the plane-trees. He was not looking for glory and immortality, as were the poets, but for a new self. Since the confident, spirited, affectionate Rodolfo had disappeared, no other Rodolfo had replaced him. Certainly, he had made a number of trial runs: a sceptical Rodolfo, a resigned Rodolfo, an immoral Rodolfo, a violent Rodolfo; but none of them had proved satisfactory. Each of these Rodolfos had no sooner settled down in his person (and he already happily saying to himself "This is me, this is the real me!") than it felt uncomfortable, on a bed of thorns. No sooner remembered, but the old Rodolfo upset everything and, although it was neither willing nor able to recover its former place, it would not allow any other Rodolfo to take over. Lord, what a wearisome business, looking for a new self! He even went so far as to envy his brother, as he had seen him one moonlit evening in the hospital garden, black-clad, at a slow jog, one hand at his back to imitate a tail, and tilting his chin sideways to emit a bray. Enzo at least felt and believed himself to be something, even if it was only a poor donkey. But he, Rodolfo, what was he now? Confident he was no longer: that was the only certainty. But can one live without identity? Certainly not. One does not live, but one suffers the tortures of the damned. He had never suspected that to be bereft of an identity, however small and humble, was such hell on earth. An identity? Each morning the sun says hullo, but to whom, to what individual? Things are all at sixes and sevens – they don't know how to behave towards one. Before dressing up in their merits and defects, before being lovely or ugly, enjoyable or tiresome, they ask: "Who are you?" Like a woman who, prior to choosing a dress to wear, asks where events may carry her. And Rodolfo did not know the answer. And things, while awaiting his answer, had nothing to put on. Everything was inane, blurred, empty. He was ashamed of himself, and at the same time afraid, because truly if Death had happened to pass close by, and had seen him thus lean, thus null and void, even though it had other things to do it would have planted a foot on him as if to say, "In the meantime I'll claim this one."

Rodolfo slumped into a bench and looked about at the sky, the whole gamut of the horizon seething above the pines and the swaying palm-trees. In this singular life which he was living, this indeterminacy, this inertia, it even seemed to him that his gaze, once it had set itself on those crests of pine and of palm, that glittering sky, on the pinnacle of the tower come into view between two trees, would nevermore come to rest within him, would remain at full stretch, from eye to tower, just as elastic when overtaxed slackens woefully and springs no longer home.

Giovanni Luisi, during the great wind, did not so much as leave the house. His suitcases – stuffed with travelling clothes, with singlets and bottles and preserves, with headache cures and books explaining the Orient to someone seeing it for the first time from the sea – had been left open-mouthed, as if choked to death by a big chunk gone down the wrong way.

He shoved them aside with his foot in the process of transporting his sleep from armchair to sofa, from sofa to bed. He was obviously never going to leave Natàca, but the idea was no longer so burdensome as before. Giovanni's inner incoherence had reached its peak now that the tower project, the only thing capable of keeping him turning, like a wheel on its axle, in the same direction, had vanished so abruptly into thin air. Giovanni not only set great store by saying that being forty was fine, ghastly, unbearable and good fun, but went even further, declaring that he was forty, thirty, twenty, fifty; that he was young, that he was an oldster, that he had his whole life before him, that it had been over for quite some time. True enough, he was never going to leave Natàca. But this thought, believe it or not, contained the other – that he was a great man; and this contained yet another, that he was unhapppy; and this, another again: that he owed himself a pat on the back and a whole heap of admiration; and this last implied that he was satisfied with himself and could sleep in peace. And indeed, he slept, and in his sleep he went on voyages. But then his slumbers became more tranquil, and even in them he voyaged no more. And the nicest vision he now had in his sleep was of himself stretched on his bed, a fist under the nape of his neck, exactly as he actually was at the instant he was dreaming it.

VIII

THE WIND had subsided and Leonardo was ambling slowly beneath the motionless trees of the Public Gardens. In the distance the tower stood in clear outline, and his thoughts started to run as follows:

"Once upon a time it took no more than a dog to bark at night, or the sound of a bucket in the well, or of the shoe that my brother in the next room dropped off the tip of his toe as he went to bed, and the joy I had within me would grow all of a sudden more intense, as when the memory of the thing that's making you happy pops back into mind brighter than ever. But what was it that made me happy, then? It was not one thing at all, but everything. In all that happened, even of the saddest, I found some secret understanding enabling me alone to realize that even in misfortune was hidden an act of infinite kindness – especially towards myself. All things were beloved in those days, but, in particular, I was. Rapt and affectionate attentions beamed down upon me from the skies, and sometimes they woke me at night and had me asking, 'Who can be looking at me like this?' The question died on my lips. What need to know where such love was coming from? Enough that it came to me . . .

"Then everything changed! For no reason. As a youth who, kept in affluence by an unknown benefactor's ample monthly remittance, suddenly discovering that the money is no longer coming and that the benefactor has vanished into thin air, must needs leave house and horses, university, servants and all, and resign himself to poverty, so I no longer found myself awakened by loving looks; nor did I any longer – and not only in misfortune but even in everyday things – discern the secret understanding that I alone knew how to interpret. I found myself forsaken, impoverished. The light was quenched! All was darkness! So what did I do? Since darkness it was, I slept. To things that have actually happened I have paid no heed at all, just as if they were dreams. Therefore when the light returns I shall be able to think of these fourteen years in Natàca as of a single night, as a single lost hour!"

These last words he not only thought, but spoke aloud to Lisa Careni, who had joined him a minute or two earlier.

"That's great!" exclaimed Lisa, "really great! D'you know what I say? That of the whole bunch of layabouts around these parts you absolutely take the biscuit!"

"Why's that, Lisa? It was dark all about me. Anything I might have done would have been equally dark! I therefore preferred to do nothing."

"You're arguing like the drunkard who got up in the morning and went and opened the cupboard door, thinking it was the window. Discovering that it was still night, he went back to bed and slept for a week, comforted throughout by the thought that the sun hadn't risen . . . All your talk about this light, this darkness, this mysterious love, this joy you've been waiting for in vain these last fourteen years . . . Well, I'm beginning to tumble to what it all adds up to!"

"Tell me all! Your innocent thoughts on the subject!"

"It's the chicken-heartedness of someone who doesn't want to do a hand's turn, who tries to throw dust in his own eyes and other people's by using long words supposed to explain why he's always in bed, and why instead of getting down to any serious work he takes it into his head to build a panoramic tower."

"Listen to me, Lisa! The day I regain that light – which is all the more mine because I have stayed faithful to it all the time I haven't had it, to the point of doing nothing and thinking of myself as dead – on that day, I tell you, I'll come and visit you, and a mere glance at my eyes will explain everything!"

"The day seems long in coming."

"Oh, I'm still young!"

"Young? Just you take a look at yourself."

And, reaching into her bag for a mirror, she placed it in his hands, which she briefly clasped in hers, at the same time giving him a direct, challenging smile. Then she turned her back on him and stalked off.

No sooner had she disappeared behind the palm-trees than Leonardo did take a look at himself in the mirror. And for the first time it came home to him that those fourteen years in Natàca were a punch smack in the face delivered for no reason by a stranger who then vanished in the crowd.

Who could this stranger be? And he, Leonardo, what harm had he ever done him, to receive such a blow from him now? Oh *he* had never done any harm to anyone! No harm to anyone ever, poor Leonardo!

"Poor Leonardo! Poor Leonardo!" This thought, becoming ever more tender and self-pitying, occasioned him much comfort, as sometimes does the humming of an appropriate air solace the lonesome road and assuage unwelcome thoughts . . . "Poor Leonardo! . . ."

Buscaino had reached Mn, the last town in the territory to which Natàca belonged. He was having a bite to eat with a friend at a cheap place near the port. There before him ended the lands of the South, among waves no longer the slumberous waves of the Lido at Natàca; amongst eyes that, if not wide awake, were at least half-open; and the sounds of an early-morning town, with people rousing themselves, clattering back the shutters, and scrubbing their chests in their doorways.

"My dear chap," said Buscaino, "no one ever manages to leave that town! I alone, perhaps. But then I am of a different mettle."

His friend eyed him with a mixture of curiosity and amusement.

"Know why I'm staring at you?" he asked. "Because you remind me of a fly just got out of the milk and barely able to crawl to the rim of the glass. So what do you propose to do next?"

"You know, I haven't the foggiest," replied Buscaino, upset by the comparison with a fly, which he felt fitted him irksomely but to a T. "Not the foggiest."

"Why don't you go back to America?"

"Hmm, not easy!" Buscaino's gaze focused on the mountains which, on the other side of the water, mingled with the clouds. "Not easy . . . Partly because I've never been there!"

And he thought. "How weird . . . I've never been to America. I've really never been there!" He glanced again at the mountains and the clouds. "It must be that I have in me a very respectable person whom I've never managed to get on familiar terms with. It's a fact that I've never entirely dared admit to myself what I have done and what I haven't. Yes, that other self of mine must be a very, very upstanding person. Me, I'm just an ordinary poor fellow. But *that* myself is anything but! . . . Now, for example I tell 'me' timidly that I've never by any stretch of imagination seen America; I do my best to smile and to make him do the same, but all he does is shake his head in a marked manner. But if instead of shaking his head, as he does now, this self of mine who is so authoritative, and without doubt highly regarded and much feared, seeing that I, poor fellow, have been so unfortunate, were to decide to take over the reins himself and put my life to rights? What about that, eh? Wouldn't that be a fine thing?"

"A penny for your thoughts," said the friend.

"Hmm."

"Beautiful, eh? Natàca . . ."

"My dear fellow! Natàca has no time to be either beautiful or ugly, concerned as it is with being tedious and gloomy. Gloom and tedium there, why, you can cut 'em with a knife.

Not a single man, not even a single bird, has ever been truly happy in Natàca, not for so much as a moment."

And with this he shot from his chair as if he had seen someone pass the door at the speed of an arrow, and it was vital to catch him. To his friend, who was still seated, with an apologetic gesture he shouted, "Sorry, but settle up, would you?"

IX

The "GIRLS" of the Pensione Orange Blossom are as restless and fluttery as the young ladies; and indeed with the young ladies they mingle at midday, when they go to partake of an aperitif at the smartest bar in Natàca, where the tuppeny-ha'penny vendors of toothpicks and coarse kitchen salt tug at the ladies' dresses and the gentlemen's jackets in an attempt to call those carefully guarded eyes to their puny merchandise. The women from the pensione are as restless as the young ladies: incapable of listening for long to the pianoforte without shedding tears or of putting up with slow service without getting cross, because they too, like the young ladies, are on the look-out for husbands among the young gentlemen of Natàca. Thus, against their wills, the young ladies of Natàca find themselves in competition with women of this kind; and the trouble is that they do not always emerge the winners. For some time now the young gentlemen have taken to spending the evenings in the dining-room of the Pensione Orange Blossom, one playing the piano, others dancing, others again in conversation with the girls, whose airs as women who have seen the world, expressed in northern accents, induce in the gentlemen a state of submissiveness that soon gives place to love. And conjugal love, at that.

For this reason the drawing-rooms of Natàca are threatened, it is said imminently, by the entry of a number of gauche but cantankerous ladies whose mouths are innocent of lipstick but broad and set, whose eyes dart this way and that but are devoid of curiosity and incapable of astonishment, at least at the things which astonish their young rivals . . . And the aforesaid young gentlemen, who go so far as to weep when at Christmas they receive from such women telegrams addressed to "my precious heart" and extolling "our blessed happiness to come", words to which they reply in even more sugared terms; these same young gentlemen, I say, ply the young ladies of Natàca with questions such as the following, recently much in vogue in the drawing-rooms:

"Do you know, miss, what creature puts a cuckold into a fit?"

"I'm sure I don't know. What's the answer?"

"A widow."

"A widow! Why on earth?"

"Because it's a fit of coffin'."

Only the other evening, in a stage box at the opera, a young man in tails removed one of his shoes and tucked it under the arm of a gentleman who had leant his elbow on the velvet balustrade. Enraptured by the music, this gentleman for several minutes kept the shoe under his arm like a book; then, making a sudden movement, he caused it to fall not only onto the stage but into the very hands which the soprano, in reaching for a high note, had turned palms uppermost.

Such, such is the youth of Natàca! Worthy indeed that the tower should be dedicated to it and henceforth known as the Tower of Youth; not least to stifle a rumour that has already sprung up and threatens to become rife, that it will be known as the Damsels' Tower . . . How natural it seems, how well in tune with the panorama of Natàca, this tower that suits the city as a finger does a glove, now that we know for certain that it is perfectly useless. Without this tower Natàca would really and truly lack something as indispensable as a nose is to a face.

Thus speak the damsels in the Careni's drawing-room as they gather around the piano, on the keys and lid of which repose a number of glasses of spirits. Taking advantage of being on their own, relieved of elder women and the menfolk, the young ladies have for the first time started drinking like fishes, as they saw some American girls doing in last night's film. They are drinking, prodding the odd note on the piano with one finger, running down men. Then come harsh words for themselves and for the lives they live. Boredom and futility, boredom and futility!

"If it goes on like this," says one, "I shall throw everything to the winds and do something desperate."

"Not really!" cries another, with concern.

The girls grow thoughtful, while the first takes a forefinger and strikes a bass note on the keyboard, then middle C, then another low note, but without managing to obtain any sound at all but "boredom and futility, boredom and futility . . ."

But all of a sudden Lisa Careni is seized with a novel and intense sensation, like a breath so deep as to expand the chest once and for all. A flush of happiness, but one quite out of the ordinary; truly something that once begun has a chance of never ending.

She grasps the bottle of spirits in her right hand, a glass in her left, and goes to the window.

In the street and on the houses the sun is shining still; the sky is clear and lucent. In the doorway opposite a woman undresses a tiny tot, lifts it naked high above her head, then lowers it onto her upturned face. As in films we sometimes see the living person move behind the mask, so behind things as they have been, vapid and drab like faded photographs, Lisa now for the very first time sees real things move, making themselves apparent in all beauty and splendour.

"Could this be the joy Leonardo talks about?" thinks Lisa. "How strange . . . He was waiting for it, but it has come to me!"

What matter? Whoever it has come to, here it is. And as someone suffering in the name of the Lord feels that all those who are dear to her and close to her are growing more and more virtuous on account of her suffering, and that little by little she is saving their souls, so Lisa, rejoicing in the name of the Lord, feels that all her friends in Natàca will become ever less surly and idle because of this joy of hers, and that little by little she will save them all. So . . . this joy, what is it? One blessed moment? Not so: there is nothing fleeting about it. On the contrary, like the sequence of a dream the moment we open our eyes, those years of wearisome fatuity, those weepings and wailings, those inanities, those dismal frivolities, that panoramic tower, all melt away; and the point at which it all dissolves into light is so steady and clear that the good Lisa thinks not only that what Leonardo said is true, that those fourteen years in Natàca are but the dream of a single night, but that even Leonardo, who thinks this way, even Giovanni, Rodolfo, Buscaino and her own advancing years and baffled affections, every scrap of it, every scrap has been a ridiculous dream now, at long last, over.

No one, we therefore feel, will raise a censorious finger if, swaying very slightly, bottle in one hand and glass in the other, our good Lisa, usually so retiring, so quiet, so shy, cries out from the window to the shimmering sky nothing more nor less than "Three cheers for life!" And this not only once but twice, three times.

Catania, November 1934–March 1936